Memoirs Of A Misfit

Escaping The Matrix

Michael Knight

North Star Publishing Inc

Copyright

My thanks to my wife Judith for putting up with me for 20 years.

And to Sherrie St James for her exceptional talent and gift of the cover art.

https://www.sherriestjamesstudios.com/

Contents

Prologue   VIII

1. God's Own Country   1

2. What's Your Name?   5

3. Birthplace Of The Gods   9

4. Devil and Satan   15

5. First Horse - First Death   17

6. Hokowhitu School   21

7. Come to Jesus.   25

8. Runaway   31

9. Fun On The Farm   41

10. Stampede   47

11. Tired Hedgehogs   53

12. Mr Goodwin - A Good Man   57

13. Warts And All   61

14. Smarter Than A Jersey   65

15. Bully Boys   73

16. Insolence + Intransigence   77

17. Sandhill Savior   83

18. Best Dad Ever   87

19. Run Me Down   93

20. Love With A Belt   97

21. Work Comes Easy   103

22. Top Of The School   107

23. School Shooting   111

24. Bully For Me   115

25. Bully For Bung   119

26. Revenge Is Sweet   125

27. On George's Farm   129

28. On Hughie's Farm   139

29. Walking On Water   147

30. A Greenstone Jewel   151

31. The Algebra Mystery   155

32. Half-brother - Runaway Father   159

33. Plane Sailing   163

34. Two On A Tandem   167

35. Love At First Sight   171

36. Follow Your Nose   173

37. Dad And The Big Freeze   179

38. Ain't Love Grand   183

39. The Manawatu Times   187

40. Dust Yourself Off   193

41. Captain Of My Ship   197

42. INVICTUS   199

43. Wellington Poofta   203

44. Motorbikes   207

45. "Where's My Bike!"   211

46. Knock Yourself Out   215

47. The Plane Truth   221

48. Star Struck - Out   225

49. Irish Wisdom   229

50. Monkey Business   233

51. Woolstore Interlude   239

52. First Up Best Dressed   243

53. The Elvis Influence   245

54. Lead Story   251

55. The Westport News   255

56. The Daily News   267

57. Celebration   275

58. Do Or Die   279

59. Epilogue   285

About The Author   287

Prologue

Welcome to "Memoirs of a Misfit."

Herein, you will be subjected to my dry humor and an occasional shard of wisdom gained through real-life experiences. Some have been good, some not quite so swell, and others have been mysteriously life-saving.

As to why the over-all theme is that of a misfit, perhaps you too have felt there is something more to life than just the mundane, everyday struggle for survival. Have you often wondered about its meaning and purpose? I certainly have, and that's the reason I felt like a misfit most of my life.

Perhaps the best definition of what a misfit is comes from a meme I found on social media. It read, "I Am A Misfit Because ... I Think For Myself."

As the saying goes, "If the hat fits, wear it," and I do believe it just might fit you too.

While I have done my best over the years to fit in, at least outwardly, inwardly, it has been a battle to escape from the matrix of group-think.

From childhood, my inner quest was to find answers to puzzling questions such as:-

"Who am I - really?"

"What is the meaning of life?"

"Where do we come from?

"Where do we go?"

The biggest question of all was, *"Who and <u>What</u> is GOD?*

However, this book is NOT about trying to convert you to anything. Your life journey is your own.

In my case, I gradually realized that I was living in a matrix of required conformity. I learned that parents and schoolteachers, employers and politicians, in fact, all people, are victims of deliberate programming, none of which provides anything close to a satisfactory answer to any of those important questions.

Many people of all persuasions did their utmost to make me fit in.

It did not work.

Granted, I have definitely screwed up more than once. Who doesn't? Fortunately, however, I have survived many events that could have killed me right there and then. Why did I survive? Perhaps to write this book is as good a reason as any.

I know there are many people seeking answers to those Big Questions, and while I have found answers that suit me personally, my sincere hope is that others will be helped - and amused - by what I share.

In a light-hearted way, this series of essays sets the stage. They are vignettes from my life up to 1963 when, after many adventures, some truly life-threatening, others quite mystical, I finally achieved my ambition of becoming a reporter. That in turn eventually lead me to America in 1990.

Until then I was destined to miraculously escape death several times in my home country, New Zealand.

Chapter 1

God's Own Country

New Zealand

BECAUSE MY BOOKS ARE selling worldwide, I believe it's important to spend a minute or two setting the stage for the adventures that follow.

New Zealand is known by Kiwis (New Zealanders) as "God's Own Country."

Where the eagle is America's iconic symbol, the kiwi is New Zealand's equivalent.

It's a flightless nocturnal little guy, a fitting symbol for one of the smallest countries in the world.

Kiwis, the human ones, are far from being as flightless as their namesake. Many thousands of them have left to make their fortunes overseas before returning home.

Many more have taken trips to hundreds of countries around the world. One, Sir Edmond Hillary, was the first (they say) to climb Mt Everest.

Some, like me, have traveled for both work and pleasure. For work as a journalist I have either lived overseas, such as in Australia, or traveled on various assignments to Britain, Canada and the United States.

Kiwi sports teams, the best-known being the rugby-playing All Blacks with their silver fern emblem, have often dominated world competitions, and yachtsmen like Sir Francis Drake have successfully taken on the best the world has to offer.

Formed by the grinding and shifting of tectonic plates and surrounded by the ocean when the great deluge of Noah's time changed the face of the earth, New Zealand was home for tens of thousands of years to a now-forgotten people identified as the Mori-Ori.

They were displaced over time by the seafaring Maori tribes, some of whom mysteriously carry DNA that has been traced to Persian ancestry. I happen to have a smattering of Maori DNA myself, along with a swag of other bloodlines.

To escape the hungry Maori, some of the Mori-Ori who on the whole were not a warlike people, built large canoes and sailed to the Chatham Islands, 400 miles east of the mainland. I have been there, met their descendants, and seen the burial sites of their ancestors among a grove of trees.

New Zealand was known to the Maori as Aotearoa (Ao-te-Aroa). I believe that translates as Land of the Long White Cloud, a reference to the fact that clouds often obscure the Southern Alps.

I was taught at school that New Zealand was home to at least seven Maori tribes by the time the Dutch explorer Abel Tasman reached its shores in 1642.

According to his log book, on his first landing he had a "bad encounter." Four of his sailors were killed when things got out of hand after he had anchored in what he named as "Murderer's Bay." At the top end of the South Island, it has since been renamed Golden Bay.

The next explorer to visit was Captain Cook in 1769. He anchored in what he named Poverty Bay, and left soon after, having, like Tasman, had a serious encounter with the local Maori, except this time several Maori warriors were killed.

Despite that, Cook would make a total of three visits to New Zealand. He meticulously mapped its coastlines and established good relations with the Maori in other locations. The notorious Cook Strait between the North and South Islands, with its rip tides and occasional extremely violent storms, is named for him.

New Zealand is both a volcanic and earthquake-prone country, and both have played a part in my life.

Being around 18,000 kilometers or 11,500 miles from England, New Zealand was the most far-flung of the British Empire's colonies.

Where the Empire had conquered other lands by force, it could not do that in this faraway island nation. Not only was it so far that it was really expensive to send troops to do the conquering and killing as they did so terribly in places like India, those they sent to New Zealand could not subdue the Maori warriors on their home turf.

This was in part because of the heavily wooded terrain into which the Maori could disappear at will, or hide in ambush, and successfully at that.

The Maori were not only skilled warriors, they were also headhunters and cannibals, and therefore a truly fearsome enemy.

Captain Cook is said to have given the Maori a pig or two, which went forth and multiplied, so much so that pig hunters and their packs of dogs now hunt for Captain Cookers - the occasional boar weighing in at several hundred pounds.

Cook's gift of breeding pigs was a boon to the Maori. Pigs make delicious eating when cooked in a hangi - a fire pit dug into the ground, followed by an animal wrapped in vegetation, covered with dirt, and left to cook to perfection for several hours.

The white men who were killed or captured by the Maori became known as pakeha (pah-key-hah), which supposedly translates as "long pig." Your imagination might help you comprehend what that alludes to.

Once Cook had done his trailblazing, New Zealand was gradually absorbed into the British Empire.

Cook was followed by whalers and sealers and settlers and missionaries. They made the months-long sea journey from Britain, bringing their sheep and goats and chickens and pigs with them. Gradually, they cleared the land to establish their homesteads and farms.

Chapter 2

What's Your Name?

I WAS BORN IN July, 1945, about 18 months after my brother Byron.

I was named William (for my paternal grandfather) Michael (for my mother's brother, Uncle Mick) and Knight (the family name).

Thereafter, I was known simply as Bill, and sometimes Billy.

I don't know at what age I first questioned the name game, but I've always had a feeling that not one of those names is "me."

What I do know is that it takes a newborn considerable time to recognize its name. The same is true of puppies, although they tend to learn their name quite a bit faster.

Call a newborn, "Billy," or a new pup "Toby," and you'll see the difference.

From the moment of birth those magnificent brains we are born with must now gather information from all the body's physical senses, and start the magic of developing intelligence, memory, beliefs, and interaction with the environment.

To do this, the brain must create something within itself to both store and recall information, such as a given name.

This is done by the development of what science calls a neuronet. This is best imagined as a spider's web or network in the brain (without the spider).

The incoming word is heard often enough that the brain sticks it to a crossing point on the web. There, it gradually grows into its own storage compartment. Whenever the brain now hears the name spoken, it automatically recognizes the word and the mind then responds.

Let's say your name is Jack, or Jill, or Bill or Billy. We hear it often enough and we naturally believe that is our name.

That's my simplistic way of saying how, as we grow, we are conditioned by our environment to believe certain things. First, we believe our name is us. We never question it.

The same is generally true of the religion or political persuasion of the family or the rules and regulations and even dress codes of the society we are born into. People generally believe and accept what they are taught or what is expected of them, without question.

Those who do eventually start questioning are quite likely to find themselves at odds with their family's traditions and beliefs, and that's how you become a black sheep, or a misfit.

It is also how you expand your mind by kicking down the walls of the box of beliefs that others would impose on you.

To believe dogma is one thing. To question and find answers (for yourself) is quite another.

Chapter 3

Birthplace Of The Gods

I WRITE THE FOLLOWING with absolutely no intention of being pretentious. I do not consider myself to be "special." These are just the facts and the truth.

I popped into this world in a small house in a small North Island town by the name of Pahiatua. That's pronounced Pa-he-ahtua.

The word is of the indigenous people, the Maori, and it translates as "birthplace of the gods."

Who?

Me?

You've got to be joking!

And what did the Maori know about gods, anyway?

My mother did not reveal my genealogy and its inclusion of Maori ancestry until I was in my 30s. She explained that the British military had failed to conquer the Maori tribes by force. Changing their approach, the British used diplomacy and subterfuge to establish treaties with the various tribes. This resulted in the gradual settlement of the country.

The introduction of Christianity, an English education system, and, of course, inter-racial marriages were all aimed at eliminating traditional Maori culture and language. This modus operandi saw the Empire eventually include over 100 countries around the globe.

The Maori tribe that some of my mixed ancestry and DNA stems from, the Ngati Kahungungu, was not as warlike as others, and, I am told, went along with the assimilation process. With intermarriage over a few generations, the Maori bloodline on my mother's side was simply not mentioned. There was no shame about its existence; it was simply not an issue.

My maternal grandmother was perhaps one fourth Maori, therefore my mother would have been one eighth, which makes me one sixteenth - plus a mix of English, French, Irish, Scotch, Spanish and, since I was born in New Zealand, I'm also a designated Kiwi. Because of that very mixed ancestry, I like to think my forebears preferred to make love, not war.

Despite the fact that I am now a naturalized American citizen, and a patriot to boot, like many immigrants, though I may never return, the country I came from will always be "home."

My paternal grandfather was Irish and a veteran of the First World War. He emigrated to New Zealand, where my father was born. He, in turn, was a veteran of World War Two, deployed for a time in the Pacific (Guadalcanal) as an airplane armorer, before returning to New Zealand and ensuring my arrival in 1945.

My brother Byron became my first buddy, and despite occasional differences of opinion over the best part of 80 years, my love for him has never wavered. The same is true of those who followed - Marie, Don, Geoff and Roger.

Although as a child I was unable to put it into words, I always felt as if I was inhabiting two worlds, the outer one being a series of sometimes mundane, sometimes life threatening or life-changing moments in the physical world.

The other and inner world can best be described as a constant mental quest in search of understanding the meaning of life. It involved deep pondering about subjects I seldom spoke about to others.

Where did I come from?

Why am I here?

What is love?

Where do we go after death?

Where and what was I before I was born?

Who or what and where is God?

As I grew up, I questioned everything in my life.

Now, at 77, I can look back with real satisfaction at having found many answers to many questions. We'll delve into some of them as we progress.

,

Like my grandfather and my father before me, I too had an opportunity to become a warrior. It was during the Vietnam war, but in retrospect, I have a suspicion that the Pahiatua gods intervened on my behalf.

In my early 20s I was a young newspaper reporter, sometimes working on the copy editing desk at the Taranaki Daily News in New Plymouth, surrounded by teleprinters pumping out screeds of articles from around the world. Many were about how the communists of North Vietnam were determined to annihilate the tens of thousands of allied troops who had been fighting and dying to save the South.

New Zealand had sent a contingent of its military and some howitzers to rain death on the enemy. The government had also introduced the draft. I missed the draft by a day.

Part of me felt disappointed because I had thought of carrying on the family warrior tradition. However, as an ambitious young reporter, I also saw an opportunity to advance my career. Yes, I had missed the draft, but as a reporter, I could volunteer to go to Vietnam as a war correspondent.

New Zealand newspapers were all members of the NZPA (The New Zealand Press Association).

You may visualize the NZPA as the hub of a spoked wheel. Using the then modern method of communicating via teleprinters, local and international news stories of interest could be quickly shared throughout the country.

As a war correspondent filing to the NZPA, your name would find its way to every newspaper hooked to the New Zealand network. The correspondent whose term in Vietnam was coming to a close when I volunteered, quickly scored a job as a Chief Reporter and eventually became the equivalent of a credentialed White House reporter. He probably finished his career as the senior reporter in the New Zealand Parliamentary pool.

My bags were packed and I was ready to go to the front lines in Vietnam when, as I say now, the gods of Pahiatua (or wherever) stepped in. The NZPA decided it was cheaper to get all their reports from Vietnam from the Reuters news agency. My assignment was canceled.

Now let's step back in time to see how experiences, some good, some bad, some life-threatening, and some truly mystical, saw me achieve my desire to become a reporter.

Let's jump into the Tardis, that blue telephone booth in which Dr Who was a master of time, to see how I, having left school the day I turned 16, with no academic qualifications at all, became a cadet reporter two years later.

The Tardis touches down shortly after my birth ...

My gold bar exploits in America would not have occurred had I not had several surprising experiences in New Zealand.

Therefore, it is essential that I set the context by relating some of those astounding events.

As a first example, my propensity for being a runaway comes to mind.

My mother was wont to recall that as a child of about three years old I was given to wandering off across the fields and through the fences around the rustic cottage in which we lived. It was just outside a small (tiny) town named Bulls (for some odd reason) and close to the Ohakea air force base where my father had trained as an armorer before going overseas. After his discharge, we moved to Palmerston North, where he established a mail run business, delivering mail and newspapers in the early hours six days a week for the next 13 years.

Getting back on track, Byron, not much bigger than me, would usually lead the way on our outdoor expeditions. However, according to my mother, I often slipped away by myself, on one occasion coming back to the cottage in a somewhat breathless state and straightforwardly telling her, "fall foo fence on picky fistle."

I don't recall being reproached for taking to the fields, squeezing my way through the lower wires of an eight-strand fence, and falling on a well-developed Scotch thistle, but the urge to go places simply to see what's there has been with me all my life.

Metaphorically speaking, I have certainly landed on many a thistle since. However, my interpretation of the term "runaway" is also much different from the conventional definition. While I might have been running from something, I was at the same time running to whatever the future might hold. Or, to filch a quote from one of those Lord of the Rings or Hobbit movies, "not all who wander are lost."

Chapter 4

Devil and Satan

I HAVE MET PEOPLE who can recall just about everything they have experienced, almost from their first breath, but I'm not one of them.

The only things I remember from the first few years of life are the occasional visit back to Grandma's place. I was two when my mother sent me to Granny's house while she herself went off to somewhere else to find me a sister, and a year later another brother, and then another, and another. Six of us inside eight years.

When it comes to having a family, my parents must have worked out what caused it because they stopped at six, there being the first-born, Byron, then me, followed by Marie, Don, Geoff and Roger.

During those absences, we were farmed out for a week or so to various relatives, friends, or neighbors.

On one such occasion, Byron and I, both under the age of five, were taken in by a neighbor a few houses down the street. We had a back bedroom to ourselves, with a window that gave us a view of the back yard and the two kennels to which two big black dogs were chained.

The first morning we woke up as the man of the house came in, loomed over us, stood us at the window and had us watching the dogs jumping and barking as they saw him there.

In a gruff voice, he told us, "That one's Devil, and that one's Satan."

A shiver ran up my back as he continued, "and they eat boys who don't behave themselves. Got that?"

While I had no idea at that age as to who the Devil and Satan might be, I just automatically recoiled at the thought of being fed to a dog who was so big and black and had such shiny white teeth.

I pondered this for a day or two, seeing the man go out to the dogs to feed them before he left for work. The dogs jumped and barked and wagged their tails every time, and he patted them on the head. They didn't bite him once. On about day four of our stay, I waited till he had left for work and sneaked out the back door. It took a certain amount of fear and courage to sidle up to one of those big, black, bouncing happy Labradors. They almost licked me to death.

I have liked, in fact sometimes loved, dogs ever since. And horses too, from the time of my first encounter with a giant Clydesdale during another of Mum's absences.

Chapter 5

First Horse - First Death

THIS TIME, I WAS sent off to a man's farm in the middle of winter. The days were short, and the nights were long. The man of the house kept his horse in an adjacent field, and as daylight began to break through the mist, he would catch and harness his horse, ready to haul a flatbed wagon loaded with hay bales to feed to his cows.

As curious as ever, one morning I followed him to the horse pasture. He opened the gate and walked toward his horse, the halter in hand as he approached the big animal, saying, "Whoa! Whoa!" as he did so.

The horse looked up from his constant grazing, took one look at the halter and man, saw the open gate, the little me standing in the middle and immediately spun on his heels, and started running toward me.

"Stop Him! Stop Him!" the man shouted.

I quickly moved to the center of the gateway, waving or more like flapping my arms like wings, yet unable to make a sound because my throat had somehow frozen shut. From the height of a tall building, the Clydesdale peered down at me, blocking his path to freedom. He kept coming, and I kept flapping - then suddenly he put on the brakes. His head disappeared from view. I looked at his huge dinner plate feet, raised my eyes to see his knees right in front of my nose. I tilted my head back and felt a gust of hot air as he exhaled in my face. His eyes looked at me first with a deadly glint that gradually softened to what I felt was a deep sense of "something" as he exhaled again, then stood quietly as his owner came alongside and presented the halter to the horse's now lowering head.

Thirty years in the future, another Clydesdale would teach me one of the most valuable lessons of my life.

Dogs, cows, sheep, horses, goats, turkeys, deer, snakes, and fish have all played significant parts in my life.

Lions too.

Such were my adventures during those times my mother went shopping for another sibling.

By the time Roger was born, I knew that babies grew inside Mum's tummy, although if I asked, she would never explain how they got there. She did say something about storks and cabbage patches, but I knew she was pulling my leg. Stork eggs don't make cabbages.

I had yet to learn about the birds and the bees, and to question the meaning of death.

It was about 1952. We were living at 82 Manawatu St, Palmerston North.

We had a chicken coop in the back yard, from which we would gather eggs, and occasionally my father would say "time to kill a chicken," and I would watch him butcher one for the table. Holding it by the legs in one hand he would lay its head and neck on a chopping block, swing the axe, then hold the chook out till it ceased its wild flapping. "It's really dead now," he woul;d say.

On what became an unforgettable moment, about 10 one morning, I was sitting by myself on the couch in the tiny living room. The sun was shining through the window behind me, keeping me warm as I studied a book I was learning to read.

It was school holiday time, probably January, and I was looking forward to visiting Grandma for a few days. My mother was on the phone in another room.

She hung up the hand-piece and came into the living room.

I glanced at her. She looked quite strange.

She spoke.

"I'm sorry, Billy, but we won't be going to see Grandma."

"Why not?"

"She's died."

My mother seemed to disappear in a dark gray mist as my little brain grappled with the imagery of my grandmother, smiling at me, gently correcting me, telling me I was a good boy and then she too faded into the darkening cloud around me. A lump formed in my throat. I squeezed my eyes shut.

In the blackness, a big question mark imprinted itself on my young mind. One word formed.

WHY?

A kaleidoscope of unsaid questions followed. Why did she die? Why do people get old? Will my mother die too? Where do people come from? Where do they go?

Gradually, the dark dissolved from black to gray to white mist as the world swam back into view. My mind filed those questions in their own locker, from which they would emerge at the most unusual times for many years to come. And each question would eventually be answered.

Chapter 6

Hokowhitu School

HOKOWHITU (PRONOUNCED HOKO-FEE-TU) IS a suburb of Palmerston North. Hokowhitu School is where Byron disappeared to five days a week, which, as a four-year-old, I had no understanding of. What did the word "school" really mean?

More than once, my mother had to come trotting down the street to catch me as I did my best to run away and find where "Bywie" was. But eventually, it was my turn to spend my first day at primary school.

The first task I was given in a smelly room full of kids my own age, and a dark haired teacher to be called "Miss Single," was one of those supposedly mind-expanding puzzle systems. It was a little two-piece unit, the bottom half having at least six geometric cutouts, into which one was expected to fit the matching wooden shape, then beat it down with a little wooden hammer.

Five minutes later, job complete, I held it up for Miss Single's approval.

She looked, smiled, turned to the others and as she did so she said, "Good boy. Do it again."

What? I did it already! Annoyed by the command that I do it again when I had already done it right, I went back to work with a vengeance, or as much as a five-year-old can muster in the way of frustration and anger. I did as I was told, hammering with gusto until she turned to me again and said, "Billy! Not so loud with the hammer."

Weekend home life was much more fun. Our father had built a high-roofed garage out the back, behind which he stacked the firewood that was required for boiling the copper in the laundry for washing day. Two concrete tubs added to that modern set-up, the tubs doing double duty as somewhere to stand the boys and wash their dirty knees.

By the time I was eight, that woodpile behind the garage naturally had to be jumped from, which I did, frequently.

The next step was to clamber onto the garage roof and jump from the lower edge. That worked great.

What next?

"What if I dig a soft patch in the garden, climb right up to the peak, and jump from there?"

What a good plan.

The soft dirt I had just dug up would make for a soft landing, or so I thought.

Garage jumps are wonderful while you're flying effortlessly through the air - until you hit the dirt and your knees are driven halfway through your chest, knocking the wind right out of you so that you can't even inhale! And when you run inside looking for help and sympathy, your mother won't give you any sympathy at all. "Well, that'll teach you, won't it?" was the best she could do.

After that, I stuck to sneaking the occasional cigarette from Dad's pack of DeRezkes. However, that too has its drawbacks (pun intended). Do not lie on your back on the back lawn and have "Bywie" light it. You just might inhale, and suddenly the fag is ejected in a wild coughing fit, only to land on your bare chest.

Ah yes. Boys will be boys. (Or at least, they used to be).

The family survived being evacuated when the nearby Manawatu River flooded that neighborhood. We returned to find the place in water up to the thresholds, a couple of dead bantams floating in the back yard, and the fire brigade using a pump to expel water from the property.

Caution. Do not wade into flood water to investigate a pump like that. There comes a point that you just might get sucked into the hole it is making, and that could be the end of you. Thankfully, as my feet started to slide out from under me, there was a fireman nearby, well capable of wading in to pull me to safety, while speaking language I would never dare use until much later in life.

What else do I recall about that school?

Girls.

There was a stand of many pine trees adjacent to the playing field. The equipment required for sports such as cricket was kept in a small shed alongside the cricket pitch. Beyond that were the pine trees, which I loved to escape to whenever we had a break from classes.

The trees provided cool and shade on hot summer days. Often I would find myself alone there, so I would take the opportunity to embrace a smaller tree trunk and lay my face against its rough bark skin. Quietly, I would try to imagine where trees came from. How did they grow so tall, and why did they smell so nice?

Came the day my reveries were once again interrupted by the school bell, calling me back to class.

My eight-year-old legs were good at running up the hill and back to class ... until two girls stepped out from where they had been hiding behind the shed.

One was bigger than the other. Nevertheless, it was two against one. In no time at all, they had me flat on my back.

Pinning my arms down, the big girl (quite good looking for her advancing age - she must have been at least 12 years old) straddled me and started kissing me on the lips.

My body's instinctive responses might have been a bit confusing, but they left me in no doubt that I was a real boy. I suspect it was telling me something about the shape of things to come.

I never told anyone about it, especially not my mother, but a worrying thought occurred.

Had I just committed a sin?

Chapter 7

Come to Jesus.

DURING THOSE YEARS IN Palmerston North, our mother was diligent about taking us to Sunday school. Religion was strong in the family - at least, some of the family.

Our paternal grandfather had been a lay preacher in the Exclusive Brethren church. However, he must have been at least a bit progressive because he left that one after a woman in the congregation was criticized for having worn lipstick to a Sunday service. He then opted for the Open Brethren, while my mother chose to adhere to the Baptist church.

She especially liked those Christian "give your life to Jesus" events that were part of the Baptist calendar to "educate" us. That's where I first heard about the God that loved me so much that he sent his own son to die for my sins.

Maybe I was a bit unusual as an eight-year-old because I couldn't really understand why a father would kill his boy to save me from whatever "sin" was, which I didn't understand either.

One such event was held during our August school holidays, mid-winter time, when the rain and cold are at their worst and night falls early in that part of the world.

For what seemed ages, the teenagers leading the event regaled us with talk about the love of Jesus. Jesus was born in a manger. Three wise men came to see him. They were guided by a star. They brought him gifts of frankincense gold and myrrh. Jesus was the only son of God. His father was a carpenter. (The only son of God but his father was a carpenter? How did that work?) He grew up and died for our sins.

All I had to do, they said, was "give my life to Jesus," and I would be "saved." I heard how I would go to heaven when I died if I "came forward." I wondered if Grandma was there in heaven? But where was "there"?

I watched other mothers nudging their children forward and giving them big hugs and happy smiles when they returned to their pew. Up on the stage they had knelt and a big person prayed over them, after which they signed a piece of paper and that was it.

My mother kept whispering, "It's your turn soon Billy," and, "if you give your life to Jesus you can go to heaven," and "Grandma's in heaven you know."

I kept my questions to myself and did the deed, but it was mostly to stop her loud whispering. She was making me squirm around as other mothers looked our way, smiling big toothy smiles as they hugged their little ones who had just been "saved."

I went forward, as they say, knelt at a chair on the stage, heard some prayer words from one of the teenage elders (Elder? Really? A teenager?) then did my best to scribble on that piece of paper, stood up self-consciously, looked out at the small sea of faces, some hugging their sons and daughters, others smiling at me for some reason.

Unaware of my inner doubts and questions, my mother was greatly pleased that I had "given my life to Jesus." So much so that when I returned to my seat on the hard wooden pew beside her, she gave me a rare hug, which was enough to make me squirm even more uncomfortably because I didn't think I was a baby anymore.

I quickly devised a way to avoid any further embarrassment by saying I needed to go to the bathroom. That facility was through a door beyond which was the church hall entrance, beyond which in turn was the great winter outdoors and the gathering dusk.

Ignoring the doors to the bathrooms, I opened the exterior door and stepped outside. The fact that I had fibbed about needing to go to the bathroom had me wondering if I had finally committed a sin. That thought quickly slipped away as I stood in the shelter of the entrance watching the rain hammer sideways, propelled by a rushing wind that temporarily subsided.

As the street lights began to switch themselves on in the gathering gloom, I found my gaze being drawn to the distant Tararua mountains, cloudless now, and above them a brilliant starry sky.

To this day, I can clearly recall my surprise at what then occurred.

Seven shooting stars flew, one after the other, from south to north above those hills.

For some reason, that made me feel special. My seven-year-old mind thought that Jesus (or his father) must be applauding me for what I had just done. After all, the wise men only had one star. I was gifted with a display of seven.

Literally, as I write this 70 years later, I am reminded of those lyrics from the Rod Stewart hit song:- "If I only knew what I know now, when I was younger."

Readers may be familiar with the annual Perseid meteor shower, and I will admit to having wondered for all these years whether what I saw was nothing but a coincidental conjunction between my "salvation" and such a natural event.

So a moment ago I did an Internet search using the Presearch search engine.

The words I used were "Perseid meteor shower New Zealand." What I learned was that "The glorious Perseid meteor shower can only be seen somewhere with a clear northern horizon, far from city lights," and that's primarily in the northern hemisphere.

However, I also discovered that there is another annual meteor shower, known as the Southern Delta Aquarids, which, though of less intensity than the Perseid event, can be seen in New Zealand every July and August. Sometimes it will peak at as many as 20, dare I say, "shooting stars" per hour.

My current semi-scientific mind is inclined to say, "right, that's what you saw. Nothing unusual or mystical about it. You were just an eight-year-old kid. Case closed."

Case closed? I don't think so. You might believe a "scientific" explanation is all that's required to dismiss an event that had a profound effect on me as a child, but you have yet to learn how many mystical occurrences have shaped my life and my relationship with God.

This next experience is not very mystical at all. But it was a life and death situation.

Our parents had taken us to a swimming hole in a river near Massey University, on the outskirts of Palmerston North. At about eight years of age, I was still learning to swim, and had no experience in fast running water.

At one point, while my father was having fun in the shallows with my younger siblings, I ventured off into deeper water. Suddenly it was too deep. My feet could no longer feel the river bottom and I was being swept downstream toward some violent rapids in an ever-narrowing channel strewn with boulders.

Flailing arms and childish gurgles as I jumped up and down and fought for air were enough to alert an angel woman who was tall and strong enough to quickly walk into that maelstrom of death. She picked me up, held me firmly to her bosom, and allowed me to put my arms around her neck, just like a little baby, as she carried me to the shore and safety.

Being a boy, I have remembered the bliss of that moment to this day.

However, an incident that has had a far more life-changing impact occurred some years later, when I was about 12 years old. It was another life and death moment. And I survived. Again. It happened because I ran away from home.

Chapter 8

Runaway

WHEN I WAS 10, the family moved to Feilding, about 10 miles from Palmerston North.

Dad had somehow been able to buy a big old house on the corner of Kimbolton Rd and East Street.

It had five bedrooms, a kitchen, dining room, and a big drawing room equipped with chairs and a piano, which my mother was quite good at playing.

"Jesus Loves me, this I know," was one of her favorites, along with "Rock of Ages."

There was a big front entryway facing Kimbolton Road, which is a significant detail for the purposes of this memoir.

Family life was punctuated with regular and often daily altercations between our parents, a consequence of which was that they now slept in separate bedrooms. Our father's was next to the one in which Byron and I had our single beds with their threadbare woolen blankets (no sheets). On a high shelf in our bedroom was a plaster of Paris mold of Springboks rugby coach Dany Craven.

The house had no insulation and single pane windows. Consequently, it was not unusual to awaken on a winter morning to see ice on the blanket where one's warm breath had frozen during the night.

This was no big deal at all. We only had severe frosts, and certainly no snowstorms or blizzards. They were reserved for the high country and the mountains and volcanoes further north on the Central Plateau. I would learn about that in a future deadly encounter with a sudden blizzard on the ski slopes of Mt Ruapehu (rua-pay-hu).

Lytton Street school was within easy walking distance, and the Feilding Agricultural High School was a short bike ride away.

The front of the property sported a big Elaeagnus hedge. It grew bigger thorns than a blackberry, but spaced further apart. A walnut tree near the East Street entrance loomed over the single-car garage.

The East Street gate, alongside the garage, was required to be closed from daylight on Fridays.

That was the day drovers would pass by, most riding horses or sitting in a horse-drawn buggy.

Stock trucks had not yet become widely used. Therefore herds of cattle and flocks of sheep, sometimes in the hundreds, were driven to the Feilding sale-yards every Friday. Most drovers had Border Collie dogs. These black and white workers were born to do what they do. They understood whistle language (provided the boss could whistle) and those who couldn't whistle through their teeth used a special piece of tin that could be just as piercing as the best. I have one in my possession to this day.

Feilding was a rural town, and I totally enjoyed living there - except for the family issues.

Our parents had fallen out of love long ago - if they were ever in love, which is debatable.

Theirs might even have been a shotgun wedding, but what do I know? I do know what a shotgun wedding feels like, but there's no need to go into detail about that.

It wasn't long before Dad had Byron and me working as paperboys. We had to be up at 5.30, six days a week.

The provincial newspaper, The Manawatu Times, would be delivered in bundles from Palmerston North to Feilding. Our job was to wrap them in glued paper covers, stow them in our canvas saddle bags, deliver them, rain or shine, then grab some breakfast and go to school.

At the time in question, Byron and I shared the same run, meaning that we did the job on alternate days, so each of us only had to be up at 5.30 three days a week.

The day I ran away was a Saturday, sometime during our six-week summer break from school, and it was my day to do the paper run. The alarm went off. I woke, feeling groggy and listless. Byron remained sound asleep.

Feeling as tired as I was, I had no desire at all to do my paper run that morning.

I had to raise my voice quite a bit to wake Byron up, then convince him that he should get up and go and do my paper run while I remained in bed for the next few hours.

Byron, eventually, though very reluctantly and with loud complaining, agreed to do so.

He dressed and left, closing the bedroom door with a loud slam as he departed.

To my horror, as I heard him exit the house, slamming that door as well, I heard a third door slam open, and then a fourth - the one into my bedroom.

There stood my very angry father. I quickly pulled my thin blankets up over my mouth, even though I knew how useless that was if he decided to pull them off me and give me a hiding. Instead, he started ripping me a new one (as they say these days) for being such "a lazy little sod" and it was "time to grow up" and "if you've got a job, it's YOUR job to do it," and "I've got a good mind to give you a bloody good hiding."

With that, he left, slamming the bedroom door shut, then the one to his own room as he took his temper back to bed.

Amazingly, I was suddenly no longer tired. I was full of energy. And resentment. And perhaps a bit of fear. Above all, I was fed up with being snapped and snarled at, which both my parents had become very good at in recent times.

My way of dealing with that, prior to this occasion, had been to slip away whenever possible across the fields to the Oroua River. There I would sit and sulk, or find myself calming down immeasurably as I sat alone beside the river, wondering where it started, what recent rains had caused its fluctuations in height and pace, and why was its water fresh when the ocean was salt?

Sometimes I would lie in the sun among the lupine bushes, watching their pods snap with a crack and expel their progeny into its new life. How do they know how and when to do that? I would wonder.

However, this time, the river was not far enough away from home. I felt I needed to go so far away that I might never come back.

I didn't need so many tongue-lashings from my father, nor any more hidings from my mother. She might profess to love me, but there is something that rings hollow when a parent says to their child, "this will hurt me more than it hurts you." That was the signal that she was about to lash out with a leather strap, or the cord from the electric kettle, or a ready-made whip of thorns she would have me cut from the Elaeagnus hedge so I might play a full part in my own punishment.

Sitting on the edge of the bed, with angry thoughts swirling around my brain, I recalled that when we had lived in Palmerston North, our parents had made friends with a family that attended the same church.

I decided to run away - a long way away.

The Christianson family were a couple who had at least three boys and a dairy farm some 10 miles or so from Palmerston North, a mile or two from the small Opiki country school.

We had visited them once when I was about eight, and now I was remembering how I had mentally recorded the way there. I often did that when we went as a family for a Sunday drive. It helped to ignore the fact that I was being crushed by five siblings in the back seat, or in the Bradford van that was a bit bigger, had no side windows, and only allowed me to see through the front window or those on either side of the front seats. I also remembered that now that we were living in Feilding, the Christianson farm would be at least 20 miles away.

As I gingerly crept off my bed, careful to do so in such a way that it would not squeak and arouse my father yet again, I recalled that I had really liked Mrs. Christianson. She was cheerful. The boys, though older than me, had been friendly. They also had a friendly dog, as well as pigs and cows and chickens, and a big garden with amazingly juicy tomatoes growing in abundance.

It took less than a minute for me to sneak out of the house, closing both doors super-quietly, then wheeling my bike out into East Street, pushing and running a few steps, then I was into the saddle and off to Opiki.

For a boy who was too tired to do his paper run, I did quite well, riding nonstop the 10 miles to Palmerston North, then a further 10 miles south out of town, following the memory map I had made on the only visit to their farm that I remembered.

With my mind set on my destination, I had to trust my gut instincts at a couple of junctions, where a bad choice could have taken me way off in the wrong direction. Fortunately, the butterflies in the stomach have their own language. They calm down once you make a decision and stick to it, whatever the outcome might be. After all, you can always change your mind and do something different.

As I passed the one-room country school at Opiki, I noticed the garden plots, one per student, were looking a little dry. Nevertheless, each plot had its array of lettuces (green and red varieties) and carrots and beets and sometimes flowers ("I'll bet they're girl gardens") which had attracted honey bees from a neighboring bee farm. It would be some years later that I would learn that a "bee farm" is really an apiary.

Taking the correct turn once again, I biked the last few miles down a gravel road till I recognized the tall compact Macarocarpa hedge behind which was the Christianson family home.

It was only in the last 100 yards of my journey that the butterflies went into overdrive. Until then, I hadn't given any thought at all as to how Mrs Christianson, or Mr Christianson himself, would react to my sudden and unexpected arrival.

As I turned into the driveway, I saw Mrs. Christianson look up from the flowerbed, then stand and face me as I stood on the brakes, hopped off the bike, planted two feet in the dust, and realized I was tongue-tied.

I think I'll reconstruct the conversation the way I'd like to remember it.

Mrs. C: "Hello!"

Me: Silence.

Mrs. C: "Who are you?"

Me: Silence.

Mrs. C: "Oh! You're one of the Knight boys?"

Me: Nod nod.

Mrs. C: "Which one?"

Me: "Bill."

Mrs. C: "Billy? Of course. Yes.

Me: Silence.

Mrs. C: "Does your mother know you're here?"

Me: Head shake. No.

Mrs. C's blue eyes turned into a penetrating look and a considerable silence ensued.

Eventually, Mrs. C: "Are you hungry?"

Me: Nods.

Mrs. C: "I'll make you a sandwich. Do you like tomatoes?"

Mrs. C disappeared into the kitchen to make that sandwich while I parked my bike against a wall and sat on the steps at the back door, observing the biggest garden I had ever seen, replete with huge tomato plants.

Behind me, inside the house, I heard Mrs. Christianson crank the handle on the wall-mounted telephone. A muffled conversation followed before she hung up and proceeded to make me the best tomato sandwich of my life. Can you imagine two slices of fresh homemade white bread, each anointed with butter she had made from their own Jersey cow cream, and a half-inch slice of lightly salted home-grown tomato? No boy who had just completed a 20-mile bicycle ride ever had such a welcome.

As she handed it to me, along with a glass of cold milk fresh from that morning's milking, she said, "I had a talk with your mother. I told her you are welcome to stay a while. She said yes."

I said nothing. A polite boy does not speak with his mouth full.

Mrs C: "Enjoy your sandwich."

Chapter 9

Fun On The Farm

AND SO BEGAN MY three-week sojourn on a real dairy farm, during which I would have an experience that has remained a personal secret to this very day.

Basil Christianson was the youngest of the Christianson boys, yet a year or two older than me. The two big brothers were their own team, so Basil was more than happy to show me the ropes on the farm.

First, he introduced me to a playful gray pup called Toby that was about nine months old. Toby was destined to play a very significant part in my young life; so much so that I would remember him forever.

I learned how to get up early and bring the cows in for milking, mustering them into the holding yard. There they would "clean out" before being cut out a few at a time and brought forward to the front yard and its eight milking bays equipped with the latest Alfa Laval milking machines.

I learned how to twist the tail of a cow, stand out of the way of a kicking back leg, and guide it into a milking stall. There I was shown how to loop a rope around the outside ankle to tie that leg so it could not kick off the cups during milking.

I became adept at holding those cups in my left hand in such a way that the vacuum was inactive until each was flipped up and onto one of the four teats on a swollen udder. Sometimes the udder was so swollen that it would already be "letting down" and dripping milk as the cups were being placed.

Gasping away to its own rhythm, those vacuum machines would extract the milk and pump it to an open vat in an adjacent room equipped with a centrifugal separator. The heavier golden cream would come out of one spout and pour into steel cream cans, which would be taken to the loading platform at the front gate. There they would be exchanged for an empty replacement can by the driver from the dairy factory that the cream would be taken to and churned into butter.

As the cream was separated out, the remainder of the milk went into nearby drums. It would then settle and turn to curds and whey which would be fed to the pigs and piglets.

In years to come, such milking sheds would be replaced by what are known as herringbone sheds, named as such because their design does indeed resemble the skeleton of a fish. They have a pit in the middle and rows on each side where many more than eight cows stand with their udders at chest height to the milkers in the pit.

Milking machines these days are much faster than those used on the Christianson farm back in the 1950s. Those early Alfa Laval machines were Model A's as compared to Ford Mustangs. The Alfa Lavals would do their best, but once their best was done, it was necessary to hand-strip the remaining milk from each and every cow before releasing her from her duty.

There is much truth in those movies wherein you see a happy boy, girl, man, or woman sitting on a stool, milking a cow and squirting milk into the face of a happy cat. Seated on a low stool and stripping a cow by hand, I would be visited by one or more of the farm cats. With practice, I could twist a tit and at least score a hit on the cat's nose. I really did that, and I must admit to some boyish glee at watching Old Ginger stagger backwards, pawing at his nose and licking his face with a muffled snarl before coming back for more.

Other things I learned included how not to think you're a tightrope walker as you try your non-existent skill atop a six-foot-high wood plank fence around the cow yard. I have since learned that where the mind is, the body follows. For the first few steps on that high narrow plank, I was fully focused on where my next step must place my following foot. It worked well for at least six steps, my arms outstretched to counterbalance my body's tendency to wobble left and right. Then, for some reason, my gaze left that rail and looked down at the ground, far, far below.

Instantly I missed my footing and fell like a stone, driving every breath from my body as it turned into a staple, upper body on one side and lower on the other side of the fence. There was a loud whoosh as my solar plexus met my backbone before I tumbled headfirst to the ground. Staggering to my feet and gasping for air, I ran like a baby to Mrs. C. up at the house.

She waited until I could blurt out some gibberish in a high squeaky voice, looked at me calmly, then, just like my mother did after that high jump off the peak of the garage, she said:- "You're a boy. You're not dead. You could try it again and get it right. Off you go." Saying which, she turned and left, throwing a parting shot back over her shoulder as she did so: "And stay off the barn roof."

What did she know about the barn roof? It was out of sight of the house and the garden where she spent her time, and I had only been up there once or twice. I did so when encouraged by my new friend to haul some electric fencing stakes with me. Sitting on the edge of the roof, looking down no more than 25 feet, we would wait for one of the many roaming free-range chickens to come by, then drop the stake, point first, off the roof. I must say I was very impressed with the way those chickens could see it leave my hands, for they were immediately a blur of squawking feathers and wings as they catapulted themselves out of danger.

If by saying I should keep off the barn roof Mrs. Christianson had shown me she was the equal of my mother, who often claimed she had eyes in the back of her head, and if any of the foregoing suggests that I was just an average boy, it should. It's just the facts of life. Boys will be boys. Or at least, they used to be.

Boys can also be as happy as a pig in mud. Especially when they get to visit a Momma pig wallowing in a sea of liquid mud, her many little piglets on the outskirts of her extended, self-made swamp.

This sow was huge. I think she was of the Landrace breed. She was one of their best, dropping as many as 12 piglets every time she gave birth.

Pigs are extremely smart animals, and she was no exception. On a hot day, she would climb into one of the many concrete water troughs on the farm. Swaying from side to side, she would force water over the edges and create a small sea of foot-deep muddy water that she intended to be as happy as a pig in.

She was a very big, very long, very well-endowed sow, with a double row of tits and nipples that were absolute magnets for her many tiny offspring.

I have no idea whether she just wanted some relief from their constant attention, but once she had struggled out of the trough, she would plunk herself down in that brown soup till her breasts had disappeared, grunting happily to herself while her children squealed and trotted frantically back and forth on the swamp's perimeter.

It was Basil who showed me how to help the piglets. He grabbed one and threw it toward its mother. It landed with a splash, and all but its tail disappeared. There's something really funny (for a boy) about seeing a piglet tail moving like a submarine periscope through the dirty little ocean for as long as it takes for a submarine piglet to reach the shore. So I joined in, tossed a piglet into the murk, then did it again. And again.

Three times was enough. All periscopes were present and accounted for, and I was feeling a bit mean about what I had done. I stopped, called to Toby the pup, and walked away.

Chapter 10

Stampede

TOWARDS THE END OF my stay at the farm, Toby and I had become good buddies. He would eventually be a well-trained cattle dog, able to respond to a whistle or two that would have him go around the cows and herd them back to the milking shed all by himself. However, as yet, he was no more than a bouncing happy chappy with about as much understanding of the world as me.

Basil had a commitment on Sundays to help a neighboring dairy farmer with the afternoon milking. He was experienced enough to handle that by himself while his brothers did the same at home. This allowed the adults to get together for their weekly tea and scones and to chat about that day's sermon. Like many dairy farmers, the neighbor had to milk his herd twice a day, seven days a week, every day of the year. Therefore, to have the Sunday evening milking handled by a responsible youngster was indeed a blessing.

On that particular Sunday, I decided to take Toby with me, find my way through several fields and fences and go and help Basil.

All I had to do was open and close a few gates on my way to the back of the Christianson farm, then scale the boundary fence to the neighbor's place. New Zealand dairy farm fences are usually about four feet high and constructed of eight strands of Number 8 wire, six inches apart, often with a run of barbed wire on top. Where the wire is loose enough, you can spread two of them apart and a well-trained dog will jump, twist its body sideways, sail through the gap like a little torpedo, then wait for you to climb over and get on with business.

I paused at the entry gate to the last field on the Christianson farm. It was a very big field indeed. Up to the right, maybe 150 yards away, was a herd of young cows and calves and a couple of black steers that I had been told were raised for meat. The boundary fence I needed to get over was about 100 yards to my left. The neighbor's field itself was empty, except for a concrete trough about 20 feet from the fence. His pigs never had access to this field, so the ground around the trough was anything but a swamp; just bare dirt where his cows had killed the grass over time.

Toby and I had already worked together to bring in the milking herd. Neither of us had any fear of cows at all. This group consisted of what Basil had told me were "replacements," which meant they were not yet old enough to be milked. They were first required to have a calf, which would start them producing milk. "You can't milk a dry heifer," Basil had said, and that made sense.

I saw some of the well-developed calves playing with each other or grazing with their mothers. I noticed one cow had her head down, grazing contentedly even though her youngster was seriously butting at her udder in order to get just one last drop of mother's milk. I couldn't tell whether he was successful or frustrated, but he soon gave her one last head-butt that almost lifted that hindquarter off the ground. Then he pranced away to join his mates in some strange game of running to nowhere, just for the fun of it.

I opened the gate. Toby and I walked through. I closed and latched the gate. "Always leave a gate as you found it," was the sage advice I had been given by Mr. Christianson. I always have, for the rest of my life.

Slapping my right thigh as the signal Toby had learned meant "walk here," we casually set off for the boundary fence. Looking into the distance, I could make out Basil in the neighbor's milking shed, twisting the tail of the last cow in the holding yard, bringing it forward for milking. He was working by himself, so although I had been a little late in deciding to go and visit, I felt good about getting there to help him strip the last few and then hose down the yards, ready for the morning milking.

Breaking free of such thoughts, I noticed I was about 75 yards from the fence as I tapped my thigh again and looked down to see if Toby was being good.

No, he wasn't.

He had decided to join those calves in their fun run to nowhere.

What neither he nor I knew was that calves are very precious to their mothers; mother cows can be quietly munching grass one second, and fire-spitting monsters the next, especially when they see a strange dog they think is about to attack their offspring. Their instant transition into a stampede of lowered heads and horns and thundering hooves scared the wits out of Toby. He spun around and started running towards me. It took but a nanosecond to assess the danger. I, too, spun around and started sprinting for that boundary fence. As I ran, I knew without a doubt that nothing on earth could stop that charge. Perhaps they would even crash through the fence. What then? Well, "if only I can jump the fence and get behind that concrete trough, I'll be safe." It was a great thought and a very good idea — but only up to the point where Toby, still in supersonic missile mode, literally ran between my legs, catching me in mid-stride, tripping me up, and sending me headfirst into the dirt.

Stunned, I sat up, turned to look at the oncoming stampede. So fast and so close were they that I could all but count the eyelashes on the low-swinging horned head of the huge black animal that was about to turn me into blood and bone.

I knew for a certainty I had no time to even stand up, let alone run.

Expecting death I shut my eyes.

Nothing happened.

I blinked.

I was behind the concrete trough.

As I sat there, totally befuddled, the stampeding animals with Toby just inches ahead of them pounded their way toward the fence. Toby got there first and dived through sideways as if he had been a grown-up torpedo dog all his short life.

Snorting furiously, the whole herd slid to a stop on the other side, all but disappearing in a huge cloud of dust as they continued bellowing their rage at missing out on the kill.

Toby stuck to my right leg like a magnet as we took the long way home, while the mystery of that experience kept my mind racing in circles. "What happened? How did I do that? Was it a miracle? Did Jesus save me? Or god himself? Or was it something in myself I didn't know about?"

Again, the answer would come much later in life.

Chapter 11

Tired Hedgehogs

MY PARENTS EVENTUALLY CAME for a visit, collected me and my bike, stuffed me in the back of the car with my siblings, and off we went back to Feilding.

It surprised me that they didn't get angry with me for running away, but I thought that might be because Mrs Christianson had told them what a good boy I had been.

For my part, I said nothing about my happy days on that first farm.

Byron was a bit less forgiving because he had had to do the paper run every morning, so it was no surprise that he had me do it every morning for the next week. I didn't complain, although I did learn that running over wandering hedgehogs on a push-bike is a very icky thing to do. It is especially icky when you do it because the dynamo-driven headlight on your bike is so weak you can hardly see the ground ahead, let alone a hedgehog.

Hedgehogs are miniature porcupines. They don't fire their needle-sharp arrows as porcupines do, but they certainly have a coat of spikes that quickly dissuade any hungry dog from snatching a quick meal. Dogs prefer their hedgehogs squashed flat by a passing car and left to warm up in the sun for a day or so. By then, it is ready as a back-scratcher and stinky odorant for a rolling pooch.

I know it's childish to remember, but here's the sort of question that Byron was wont to come up with.

"Why didn't the hedgehog get across the road?"

"I dunno."

"Because he got tired."

"What?"

"Tired. You know, tired."

"Hedgehogs don't get tired."

"Yes, they do."

"They don't."

"They get car tired."

Me - silence. Then a snigger.

What I do not recommend is trying to save a hedgehog from getting tired, either by your bike or by a passing car. Never try kicking him off the road and onto the verge as you pass by in the rain on your early dawn paper round.

Especially you should not do that while wearing open-toed Roman sandals. Those spikes hurt like hell, while the hedgehog whose life you have just tried to save is sailing through the air, having instantly rolled himself into a prickly ball, which is their natural defensive habit.

I watched him hit the ground and bounce into the fast-flowing gutter.

Can hedgehogs swim? I don't know. I had to finish my paper run, get home for a Weetbix breakfast, then go off to Lytton Street School.

Chapter 12

Mr Goodwin - A Good Man

L YTTON STREET SCHOOL IS where I was introduced to rugby and cricket, met some bullies that I would have to deal with then, and in future years, and had my first taste of politics.

Being a gem in the empire of The Crown, many places in New Zealand were named for those who had served their masters well. Feilding, for example, was named for some bloke whose exploits I can't be bothered looking up. On the other hand, Lytton Street was named after a past British politician and Secretary of State for the Colonies, Lord Edward Bulwer-Lytton (1803 - 1873).

As an aside, and perhaps coincidentally, I have since discovered, thanks to Britannica, that Lord Edward Bulwer-Lytton - "was also a well-known writer. He originated the popular opening line *'it was a dark and stormy night'* in his novel *Paul Clifford*, as well as the famous phrase *'the pen is mightier than the sword'* in his play *"Richelieu; Or the Conspiracy."* Another source says "he also gave the world the memorable phrase *'pursuit of the almighty dollar'* (and) he is widely credited for *'the great unwashed.'*

I have used them all over the past 65 years. In fact, the subtitle of my current Rumble and BitChute video channels that are titled Knightbeat News, is a play on one of Bulwer-Lytton's originals:- *"My Pen Is My Sword."*

The only Lytton Street teacher I remember was Mr Goodwin. He drove a racy two-door copper-brown Jowett Javelin, taught us arithmetic and English, smoked a pipe during breaks, and took me under his wing. Perhaps he did that because he and his wife had no children, or perhaps because he had heard gossip about my parents' constant arguing.

Whatever the reason, he spoke with my parents and I was asked if I would like to do some lawn mowing and gardening chores at his place at weekends or during school holidays.

How could a 12-year-old say "No"?

The Goodwins owned an impressive two-storied Tudor-style mansion on five acres. They had planted an orchard, created a rather extensive garden and fenced off an acre or two of pasture for a Jersey cow, which he milked by hand every morning. The rabbits just came with the territory and sometimes into the pot.

At Lytton St school, teachers had their own classrooms and students would move from one to another at 45-minute intervals. The day would usually start for me with my first class under Mr Goodwin's tutelage. First break would see hundreds of kids descending on the milk stand where a half pint of milk was available for each of us. Hot days and warm milk going sour in its half pint glass bottle are definitely a recipe for a lifelong memory. I quickly learned to hold my breath and drink without stopping. This meant I only had to taste the sour smelling stuff once. A few years later, and for many years to come, I adapted that habit when drinking the first beer. I would upend the first 8 oz glass, drink it non stop, and after that, they all tasted great.

Mr Goodwin had high expectations of all his students. He never skimped when it came to doling out homework. Reading was important, as was the writing of a short essay as homework assignments on whatever subject he had required us to read, contemplate and write about. While we were also expected to practice and learn the 12 multiplication tables by heart (which I did) writing was by far my favorite subject.

There is no way that I can claim to have been a gifted student. I did not particularly like being in a classroom surrounded by 30 or more noisy boys and girls. Whatever Mr Goodwin and teachers in my later high school years might have tried to teach me about the structure and use of the English language must surely have gone in one ear and out the other. If they spent any time trying to drum into me the understanding of nouns, pronouns verbs and adverbs, I have absolutely no memory of it - or them.

Nevertheless, I enjoyed writing, and I even had more than a modicum of interest in arithmetic, to the extent that I was looking forward to getting into more advanced mathematics at high school.

However, there was an experience at Lytton Street that truly had a major impact on my thinking about the mysteries of the mind.

Physical education, or PE as it was called, was a big thing in New Zealand schools in those days.

Like the daily half pint of milk, nutrition and exercise were understood to be essential to the good health of developing teenagers. There was an outdoor basketball court, pull-up bars, and overhead "ladders" for us to swing from one rung to another. They do this in the military all the time. Aside from playing rugby and cricket, there was an emphasis on gymnastics, track, distance and cross-country running, tennis, volleyball, outdoor basketball and at some schools, an annual boxing tournament. I participated in all of them.

Chapter 13

Warts And All

THERE WERE ALSO A couple of rustic squash courts at Lytton Street school.

The game was very much like indoor squash, but was played with bare hands and a tennis ball.

It required a court of three walls, in this case made out of concrete blocks. The objective was to hit the tennis ball as hard as possible with an open hand, aiming it above a painted white line which ran around all three walls. I was very good at mentally computing a trajectory which would often cause my opponents to miss the ball and it would sometimes fly right out of the open side of the court.

As I was moving into my teenage years, I was beginning to grow taller and stronger and faster. However, for some reason, as my body was changing, my hands developed many unsightly warts. They didn't inhibit my squash playing in any way, but they surely were as ugly as sin. By my count, and this is a fact, there were a total of 52 of them on my two hands, mostly on and between my fingers.

I don't remember exactly what the procedure was, but my parents took me to a local doctor who spent some time removing the warts on my right hand. It was a painless process because he first "froze" the wart he was working on before cutting it out. When finished, he bandaged the hand and told my parents to bring me back once it was healed and he'd do the other one. My left hand still had about 25 warts on it.

Despite the throbbing that developed beneath the bandage, I was able to hold a pencil between thumb and forefinger and stoically got through the next day's morning classes. At lunchtime, I sat on a bench near the squash court, studying the techniques of the various players while working out how to defeat them in future games.

After a couple of bites of my soggy lettuce and tomato sandwich (they're horrible), I stood up to head for the garbage can.

Two steps later, a very fast tennis ball that had bounced off one of the court walls came whizzing in my direction. My reflexes kicked in. Right-handed, I slammed it back to the court.

The pain that instantly flooded through my right hand was incredible, but I didn't make a sound. Left-handed, I wiped the tears from my eyes. Then, as my eyes opened, I saw the welling stain of bright red blood oozing through the bandage on my right hand.

There are times when words are useless when it comes to expressing the full impact and power of a thought. This was one of those times. The best I can say is that with all the inner power and passion at my command at the age of 12, I wanted all my warts gone, gone, GONE!

Within a week, scar tissue had sealed over where warts had been removed from my right hand.

And all those on my left hand had simply disappeared.

I wondered about that for many years.

Chapter 14

Smarter Than A Jersey

Having taken me under his wing, but careful to show no favoritism in class, Mr Goodwin would congratulate me on doing my homework, and sometimes have me recite such things as the 12 times table. I wondered, but never asked, why we stopped there. Shouldn't we go on to 13 x 13?

Mr Goodwin was in the habit of coming outside during our morning break. I remember watching, quite fascinated, as he would open a small can of Zephyr tobacco from South Africa, take a flake and place it in his left palm, then pull a straight-stemmed pipe from an inner pocket of his jacket. He would fill the pipe, light it with a Beehive match, and stand there puffing contentedly until it was time to resume class.

As summer came on, probably in 1957, we were due for the annual six-week break. I had spent some days during the Spring at the Goodwins' mansion, digging the garden in which he would plant potatoes, carrots, red beets and chard. It is known as Silver Beet in New Zealand, although it looks nothing like a beet at all.

For Mrs Goodwin, I planted flowers, bright red Zinnias being the only ones I remember. The seeds quickly became long-stemmed red flowers, standing erect like a platoon of soldiers. In a warm summer breeze, they would gently move their heads in unison from side to side. Watching them in full bloom, I would stand entranced, wondering how tiny seeds know how to become whatever they are destined to be. The unspoken question was, how is it that everything starts from a seed, including me?

On the last day of school before our six-week summer break, Mr Goodwin asked me to be at his place by 7 the next morning. Up till then, a 9 o'clock start had been the rule. He explained that he wanted me to watch him milk his Jersey cow, which was his first chore of the day. "It's something you should learn," he said. Thinking there was no reason to boast about having hand-stripped dozens of cows on the Christianson farm, I said "Yes sir," and I was at his place right on time the next morning.

I was impressed. He emerged from the small detached dairy room where he had donned his oversize milking jacket. In one hand, he held his milking stool and, in the other, an empty metal bucket. He had me stay at the gate while he walked into the paddock, casually approaching the nearby cow. Setting the stool down on her left, he placed the bucket under her udder and began milking. They were close enough that I could study what he was doing. The cow just stood there, quietly taking an occasional bite of grass, then chewing her cud while he performed the daily ritual. In a few minutes, he had all but filled the bucket with the four or five gallons of milk she had turned the grass into in the last 24 hours.

That done, we returned to the small dairy where he had a hand-cranked separator. Putting aside some whole milk in a big glass jar, he showed me how to assemble the separator. Next, he poured the rest of the whole milk into the big bowl on top, cranked the handle for a few minutes, and soon there was cream for making butter in one clean bucket and skim milk in the other. Unlike the Christianson farm with its 100 cows to milk morning and night, and pigs to grow fat on the curdled whey, Mr Goodwin simply poured the whey down the drain.

He turned to me and, looking down from his impressive six-foot height, asked, "D'you think you could do all this? Milk her and separate the milk. Wash up and keep things clean?"

Me? Do all that? Of course I could. I was a cow milking veteran, wasn't I? I had stripped hundreds of cows when I ran away to the Christianson place, hadn't I? So what was the big deal?

"Yes sir."

"Could you do this every day for a few weeks?"

"Yes sir," I replied, somewhat puzzled by the question.

"Mrs Goodwin and I have a holiday cottage up near Whangarei," was his next comment.

I knew from geography lessons that was way up north, about 500 miles.

"And we like to spend a few weeks there during the summer holidays."

It was becoming a little clearer.

"Yes sir."

"I'd like you to milk the cow while we're gone. Could you do that?"

"Yes Sir!"

"And of course you can keep the cream."

I almost drooled at the thought of cream on Weetbix, or porridge, smothered in sugar.

And so it was that a few days later they left, and it was my job to get to his place no later than 7 o'clock and milk the cow.

I was out of bed early, dressed quickly, jumped on my bike and a mile or so later, I was on the job. Bucket and stool in hand, I deftly opened the gate to the cow's pasture, closed it behind me, and quietly walked toward Daisy. Believe it or not, her name really was Daisy. Doing exactly as Mr Goodwin had shown me, I approached rather slowly, dropped the stool alongside her left back leg ... and she walked off.

I waited till she stopped a few yards away, put her head down, took a bite of grass, and started chewing her cud. Carefully, I picked up the stool, walked over to her... and she walked away.

Rinse and repeat, as they say.

The third repetition of this scenario was enough to convince me that this wasn't going to work. So what to do? How was I to outsmart a smart Jersey cow?

Bucket and stool in hand, I left the paddock, taking myself out of her sight. I had a plan. It was obvious that she considered me to be a stranger, which for an animal is all about "Stranger! Danger!"

Back in the dairy, my plan really started coming together. Hanging from a nail on the wall was Mr Goodwin's milking jacket. I took it down and put it on, noting the faint odor of pipe tobacco smoke as I did so, and thinking to myself, "Good!"

The jacket was a lot bigger than I expected. It was heavy and came down to my knees. But I was still able to walk back to the paddock, bucket and stool included, then stand at the gate and watch old Daisy from a reasonable distance. More importantly, I was watching the breeze ruffling the grass she was pursuing. Satisfied with what I observed, I made my way to a point where I was upwind from her.

Once again, I approached quietly, set the stool down by her left rear leg, sat down, placed the bucket under her udder... and within a few minutes, the bucket was full. And she hadn't moved a step.

Obviously, the smell of that jacket and the pipe smoke odor had done the trick. It was a great plan. It also had me wondering about smoking a pipe myself, and therein lies a small diversionary tale.

There was a small block of shops in the small town of Feilding. Therein my dad, who had done his apprenticeship as a boot-maker many years ago, opened his own store.

Behind those premises were the long-drop latrines, and a block away was one of the original stores in the Woolworths chain. Its profusion of knick-knacks functioned like a magnet to us kids. We'd browse through them on Friday nights when shops were open till 8 pm, rather than the normal 9 to 5 and closed on weekends.

Woolworths was one of my favorite places. One had to be careful not to touch things or pick them up because the rule was "if you break it you buy it." I would wonder what this and that was there for, and what use I might put it to, which included a selection of pipes.

Mr Goodwin's manner of smoking a pipe, and my father's roll-your-own style of making smokes, had me secretly wishing I was a big man. Knowing my father had a lot of money - the till was always full of coins so he must be rich - I sneaked a half-crown when he wasn't looking. In his jacket that hung behind the door to his workshop, I found a pouch of tobacco and nabbed a pinch or two of that and a box of Beehive matches. A quick trip to Woolworths followed. I bought the pipe I had had my eye on. "My Dad said I could," was all the owner needed to hear.

Rather than go through the front door of Dad's shop, which would be a complete disaster, I used an old back alleyway and soon I had locked myself into one of the out-houses. Using Mr Goodwin's technique of placing a pinch of tobacco in his left hand, I did so, then upturned the pipe, rolled the bowl over the tobacco, and within a minute, it was nicely packed to the brim.

Next, I put it between my teeth, lit a match and then the pipe.

Pipes come in a wide variety of configurations. My favorites these days are the Peterson System pipe, or their Aran Rusticated Fishtail.

My first pipe, however, was one of a kind. The tobacco took on that bright red evidence that it was on fire.

Convinced that I was well on the road to being a man, I sucked in the smoke.

Within an instant I was gagging and ready to throw up as I watched the edges of the bowl catch fire and begin to melt red lava into that mini volcano of red-hot tobacco.

I haven't smoked a plastic bubble pipe since.

Chapter 15

Bully Boys

THE NAMES OF NEIL Billett and Bryce Dunn have stuck with me forever. That's because they were bullies.

There were others back then whose names escape me, but according to myself, it was my job to deal with them. This I did, either spontaneously in a moment of righteous anger, or in a cold-blooded manner, when the right opportunity presented itself.

For instance, at Lytton Street during a recess, a number of us had been out on the rugby field practicing scrummages or goal kicking. The bell rang to call us back to class, and right then, I saw Billett barge into an unsuspecting student, smashing into him from behind and dumping him to the ground.

I watched, expecting no more. But then Billett jumped in the air and, with his rugby boot with the sprigs on the sole, landed on the other boy's head.

It was payback time. Without thinking at all, but driven by a sense of fury, I ran like an All Black winger, tackled Billett, and slammed him to the ground. I stood up, raised my booted foot and, with no intention of following through, I waved it over his shocked face. I couldn't believe it. He started crying.

I walked away.

Bryce Dunn was another one. He got his comeuppance at the Feilding sale yards. That was a huge complex of cattle and sheep pens and a circular indoor auctioneer's arena where sellers and buyers would attend the weekly sale or the annual offering of stud rams from the many topnotch breeders in the district.

The annual stud sale would go on for days. Hundreds of big rams would be kept in undercover pens, and boys would be employed to drive them to and from the arena. Those rams could weigh as much as 200 pounds, as compared to a boy's weight of around 100.

The rams were feisty and dangerous. Therefore, each boy was supplied with a short heavy rope, knotted at one end. Its purpose was to drive the ram forward, or to bang him in the head if he chose to have a go at you.

Bryce Dunn and my two youngest brothers, Geoff and Roger, were working at that year's sale. Geoff was no more than 12 years old, and Roger was perhaps 11. When they got home from their first day on the job, they showed me the welts on their arms and backs where Bryce Dunn had whipped them with his knotted rope as they passed each other going to and from the arena.

That night, I hatched a plan. I figured that most of the adults would be in the arena, so they'd never notice a new boy on the job. Next morning we arrived in time to join the throng of boys ready for another day's work. I grabbed a knotted rope and settled into the job without any of the men noticing at all.

An opportunity for vengeance soon presented itself. Bryce Dunn was driving a ram back to its pen while I was shunting one toward the arena. As we passed, I whacked him several times as hard as I could.

"Want more?" I asked through gritted teeth. A cringing shake of his head was enough of a response. It was game over. Or so I thought. We would meet again when we were a few years older.

Chapter 16

Insolence +
Intransigence

W HEN YOU'RE A KID, it seems that adults are only okay, up to a point.

My experience in the beginning stages of Boy Scouts, and later in the Boys Brigade, was that most of those in a uniform or any position of authority, just love to demand that you do what they say.

I was always okay with that, provided they asked in a reasonable tone of voice, and provided also that I agreed with the request, or order. And therein lies the answer to why I was considered by some in uniform to be an insolent boy.

They didn't understand that they should ask me to do something in a nice way. They should have also understood that if they started demanding or talking down to me, my hackles would go up. I would dig in my heels, and they would have to deal with a kid who just wouldn't do as he was told. (Serve 'em right).

Boy Scouts was a big thing back then, although to become a Boy Scout you had to first attend weekly meetings of a subgroup for kids aged about 9 to 11 known as Cub Scouts. In the dead of winter, these gatherings would be in a church hall about two or three miles from our home in Palmerston North. Two or three miles was no distance at all for a kid on a bike with a weak headlight driven by a dynamo working off the front wheel. It was so powerful you could see maybe 6 ft in front of you on a dark and stormy night.

I only made it through about three such Cub Scout events.

The teacher, who we were required to address as Ahkayla for some dumb reason, because that wasn't her real name, was a woman in a uniform. I did not like her tone of voice at all, especially when she always seemed to be telling us to line up, and to salute her and say "Yes, Ahkayla" whenever she spoke to us personally. My saluting must have been pretty sloppy because she definitely raised her voice at me - to which I responded with some cheeky remark that she did not like at all.

The third week, my mother picked me up in order to save me from that long bike ride home in the cold and foggy wintry dark. "Ahkayla" said something to her in that secretive way that adult women have when they don't want the kids to hear. I found out what it was when we got in the car. Mum said I had been very insolent, and I was no longer welcome at Cub Scouts. It didn't bother me a bit. I knew I had not been insolent. I might have raised my little voice just a bit, but that was only because I had to match Ahkayla's tone when I asked a very legitimate question, "Why do I have to salute you? You're not my mother."

It was a fib on the spur of the moment, because I never had to salute my mother at all, and I may, late in life, finally be getting over that dislike of being spoken to in a demanding or controlling tone of voice. That's because, very slowly, I have discovered a similar fault in myself. Some have said that we only see in others what exists in us; they are but a mirror, and if we don't like what we see in them, it's time to deal with that in ourselves. I take that to mean birds of a feather tend to flock together - our acquaintances reflect our emotions, our feelings, our attitudes and thoughts.

On another occasion, years later, refusing to salute got me a kick in the butt, literally. My father started the Feilding Boys Brigade group for the benefit of quite a few local teenagers, including my brother Byron and one of his friends. Byron had a way of being friends with older boys I had no liking for. It tended to be mutual. They didn't like me either. Hindsight again tells me I was envious and even jealous, but I had good reason to detest one in particular who would pick on me without reason whenever Byron was out of sight.

I forget his name, or I do not care to remember, but my way of dealing with him was to act like a cocky little prick, call him names and baffle him with big words that would get him as mad as hell - until one day, he just couldn't take it any more.

What say we just refer to him from here on as "Big Boy."

For some inexplicable reason, my father promoted Big Boy to the rank of NCO in the Boys Brigade. Although I don't recall Dad wearing a uniform himself, he certainly had a military background, a military bearing, and a military way of speaking. We boys, or troops, had to "Fall IN!", "Right TURN' and "quick MARCH!" around the hall.

Then it was "HALT!"

"Face FRONT!"

"AttenSHUN."

A short pause, then "at EASE" and we'd take the stand easy position, waiting for the next instructions, whatever they might be.

Calling Big Boy out by name, Captain Dad announced that Big Boy had been promoted to company NCO - and we would, from now on, be required to salute him whenever requested.

It didn't work for me. Was I expected to salute this fat overweight oaf who liked to pick on me all the time? Not a chance.

Inevitably, there came a moment, just a few minutes later, when the new NCO stepped out front as ordered and we were instructed to salute him.

I did not.

The captain's voice took on that parade ground tenor, loud enough to be heard well outside the walls of a church hall.

At least three times I was ordered to salute, Dad's voice getting louder every minute as I just stared him down with what he knew from home experience was my most recalcitrant demeanor.

Suddenly, the Boys Brigade Captain in the church hall turned into a father who was utterly angry and embarrassed (I guess) by his son's refusal, in front of all the others, to salute an NCO.

In two swift steps he was at me, saying "Learn some respect BOY!" as he spun me around, threw me toward the open door, and planted a kick in my butt that, if he had been the goal kicker for the All Blacks, would have put the football right between the posts from fifty yards out.

I don't think my feet touched the ground before I landed, hard, on the outside concrete path. I swear I could hear the sudden absolute silence back in the hall where even the NCO was looking at the four-star general with a new respect - tinged with fear, no doubt.

But not me. What's to fear about a stupid Big Boy NCO? And as for Dad, he'd get over it in a day or two. So would I. We always did - although sometimes it would take years.

Chapter 17

Sandhill Savior

O NE OF THE BEAUTIES about New Zealand is that the beaches are, for the most part, easy to reach.

It certainly has an awesomely rugged coastline in some places, with many fjords on the South Island's West Coast being inaccessible except by boat or helicopter (been there, done that). However, in under an hour's drive from Feilding, the Manawatu River meets the Tasman Sea. The sandy beach stretches for many miles. The small township of Foxton Beach boasted a store, a Post Office, and numerous beach houses in which dentists and doctors and my grandfather spent holidays and long weekends. For those not in the upper income bracket, there was a campground. Boys Brigade troupes from various towns would get together there once a year, set up surplus army tents, and generally have a great time on hot summer days.

Although I was never required to salute that NCO again, my father and I had got over that incident by the time we were camping at Foxton. In the interim, I had befriended Ivan Horbun, a Feilding boy of my own age. His mother owned the Feilding Hotel, but his father was long gone. We were both in the Boys Brigade and were all but inseparable during the week at the Foxton Beach camping event. We also got together at other times. One memorable event involved a couple of stolen cigarettes that I lifted from my father's jacket at his shoe repair shop. Ivan and I then made our way to a big old barn beside the Baptist church where we all but made ourselves sick by doing the drawback. We both carefully stubbed out our fags and prepared to leave when we noticed a big, old burn barrel. It was a cold day, so it seemed logical to fire up the barrel and get warm. No sooner said than done.

It did not take long for the contents of the barrel to burn away, so we diligently picked up a few clods of dirt and threw them into the barrel to ensure the fire went out.

I woke the next morning to the sound of my father's voice commanding me to "Come here!"

He was sitting up in bed reading the morning paper.

"Did you do this?"

"Do what?"

"THIS!" he said, revealing a front-page picture of a burned down barn.

Y'know, telling the truth should have its limits, like when telling the truth is going to be used against you. In such times, a half truth or a return question can deflect the inquisitor, but it takes hard real-life experiences to get to that point.

I blurted out something like, "But we put out the fire in the burn barrel."

"You did, did you? And the cigarettes?"

Before long, my ear was being held in his vice-like grip as he walked me to the local police station. There a policeman twice my father's size and height towered over this kid, who was determined not to start blubbering.

My father confessed on my behalf to which the cop responded that lacking first hand evidence a confession was not sufficient to have me sent off to a home for bad boys. However, he said, he would show me where I might end up if I continued this sort of behavior.

Both he and my father seemed to agree that I needed to learn something else about possible futures.

Some say that iron bars do not a prison make, but I am here to tell you that being locked in a police cell for just a few minutes can be enough to straighten out any wayward youngster. I'll never forget the sound of that iron door slamming behind me as they shoved me into one of the two cells in that small police station.

A few minutes in there was enough to convince myself that I would never get caught again. To my credit, however, I never said a word about my friend Ivan having been involved in the escapade as well. Nor did I know then that we would share yet another close call, this time during a Boys Brigade camping trip at Foxton beach.

After a spell of rain Ivan and I went cave digging in one of the steep sandhills. It was probably 50 feet high with a relatively sheer face. Starting at the base, we began burrowing out a tunnel in the wet sand with our bare hands, taking turns lying on our bellies, shoveling sand back behind us and getting deeper and deeper.

Before long, only my ankles were out in the daylight. Without warning, the whole thing collapsed on top of me. Instantly I pulled my elbows together, raising my back at the same time, knowing I had to create an air pocket as best I could if I were going to survive - or not.

Realizing that Ivan could not hear my voice, I mentally "shouted" at Ivan, "Do NOT go for help. Dig me out!"

There was a long silence during which I feared he may have panicked and headed back to camp for help. In fact, he had been furiously digging into the landslide of sand, trying to find my feet. Working frantically, he moved what felt like several tons of sand off my body until he was able to pull on my legs and haul me back to daylight.

Ivan saved my life.

Chapter 18

Best Dad Ever

ALTHOUGH WE HAD OUR occasional altercations, including on one occasion a fistfight almost to the death, my father was a good man, a hard-working man, a man who would work 18 hours a day seven days a week to bring home the bacon - not that we ever had too much of that.

To call him the best dad ever is a truth. Considering he was my only one, it is also a play on words. Even the best of fathers have their bad days. This incident was one of those.

On the corner of Kimbolton Rd and Lytton Street was a small mom and pop dairy. They were neighbors, but by no means friends. It was convenient for my father to buy cigarettes there, or occasionally send me over to get some for him.

As a quick aside, I once also bought a stick of chewing tobacco, fibbing about how Dad had changed his habit. Back home, one chew on such compressed tobacco set my head spinning and my stomach churning so badly I fell to the floor. I recommend not ever swallowing chewing tobacco. Not that I ever bought any more thereafter.

Now back to that incident, which turned into what I have previously mentioned as a fight to the death.

I was in the front entranceway listening to Randy Stone on the radio. He had just finished his "I cover the night beat for The Daily" line, when my mother came flying out of her bedroom, screaming incoherently. Wearing only her pinkish, wildly flapping nightdress, she ran down the steps and across the road.

I stood there in shock. For the first and only time ever, I wondered what the neighbors would think.

The next second I heard my father, out of sight behind me, say, "Stupid woman!"

In a trice, my right fist was almost at floor level. I spun to my left and with all my might delivered an uppercut that, I swear, lifted him off the floor.

Did I mention that my grandfather had been a British Empire middleweight boxing champion?

And that my father was a WW2 veteran.

And an All Black rugby team trialist?

And that when his feet hit the floor again, it was all on - nonstop, blow for blow, both of us consumed by frustration.

What little boxing I had learned enabled me to feint and jab and punch with great effect. (Liar. I would have done better hitting a concrete post).

The fight went on, it seemed, forever. We fought in the entryway, transited to the hallway, and then to the room where the piano offered me a safe place to back between it and the wall.

By then, my nose was sideways, I had a tooth through my bottom lip, and my left arm had been hit so many times it was getting harder and harder to throw any jabs and feints, let alone any solid punches.

He, too, was showing signs of being a wounded warrior. Yet I knew instinctively that he was starting to get control of his temper, and I of mine.

As he backed away and paused, ready to come at me again, I looked him in the eye and said, meaning every word of it, "If we keep this up, one of us will go out of here dead."

The fight ended there and then.

I must add that I still have no idea what set my mother to her fit of histrionics. I do know she was never physically abused by my father. Years later he would confide in me that there were times in their younger days when, in bed together, he would be asleep and she would prod him with a hat pin and demand sex.

Did he comply?

I never asked.

But I'm here, am I not ... and if you'll forgive my wry humor, maybe that's why he sometimes used a favored Kiwi expression, calling me a "little prick."

Regardless of that bruising fight we had, my father still deserves the title of Best Dad Ever, and here's just one of many reasons why.

Americans are quite familiar with those trailers that are outfitted as mobile kitchens, offering hot dogs and burgers at fairs and gun shows.

Sixty years ago, Dad and I worked in something similar on Saturday nights in Palmerston North. It was known to us as a Pie Cart, a caravan set up to dispense take-away (or takeout) meat pies, or sit-down meals of hamburger and chips (french fries) at a small counter at the rear.

It was known as the place to grab a feed on Saturday night. I soon became adept at mixing hamburger meat with eggs and flour, shaping them to the right size, cooking them on the grill while timing everything so the burger and chips and sometimes an egg or two were "just right" when handed to the customer at the sit-down counter.

As for pies, they were freshly made each day at home by the owner, filled again with hamburger (we called it minced meat) or stewed steak, peas, carrots and gravy.

Customers would ask for a "pea pie and pud" and we'd give them a brown paper bag containing a pie of their choice topped with a big dob of buttery mashed potatoes and a spoonful of dried green peas boiled and mashed into a paste that to this day I recall as having an unforgettable flavor.

Something I had not discussed with my father was the gang of five boys who, for the last couple of years had taken delight in surrounding me whenever they found me on my own, threatening to knock me off the planet, and laughing at my apparent refusal to fight.

I didn't retaliate because I was still under the sway of my mother's admonition to "turn the other cheek," which I did religiously (almost) until I was 17. I was only 16 on this particular Saturday night when three of the gang suddenly seated themselves at the end counter.

Not knowing who my father was, they ignored him while loudly focusing on me as I readied their order of burger and eggs.

"Look at the sooky boy!"

"Hey, you - we'll get you yet."

"Oi! 'ow about a punch-up?"

I kept my mouth shut as I flipped their burgers, although seething inside while doing my best to stay calm and let their insults wash over me like water off a duck's back. Well, it turned out that my father was no duck.

In one smooth movement, he reached under the counter, grabbed a wooden club in his right fist, slammed the butt down in front of my tormentors, and snapped at them:- "He's my boy. Now shut up and behave. Or get out and go home."

Sudden silence filled the Pie Cart.

I couldn't stop myself from smiling a sneering smile at all of them as I served their meals, although I had a feeling we would meet again, and my father would probably not be there to protect me.

There would come a time spanning many years during which I had nothing to do with either of my parents. However, as I matured and became a little older and wiser, on my own birthdays I would send both of them a card of thanks for bringing me into this world.

Yes, there were times that I self-righteously blamed them for my own faults, but that ended when I learned that while they were responsible for my birth, they were never responsible for any of the choices I made.

Everyone is born with free will, and that means it is we, not others, including our parents, who make the choices (good or bad, wise or foolish) that create our lives. It is now my understanding that some of my own unwise choices, about which I have no regrets, were essential in developing such wisdom as I now have.

Chapter 19

Run Me Down

A FEW YEARS LATER, the gang had acquired a 1938 4-door Ford, a big car with step-on running boards and a loud engine.

In New Zealand, the steering wheel and controls are on the right of the vehicle. (That's a significant point in regard to what follows). I was meandering alone along the shore at Foxton Beach. The tide was out, and the sand was firm so beach-goers could drive for miles in either direction.

My reverie was suddenly broken when I heard the familiar sound of a car revving up behind me. There was no mistaking the sound of that V8. The gang!

Quickly looking over my shoulder, I saw plumes of sand flying up behind their car as they accelerated toward me. The driver's face was clearly visible through the windscreen, his brow furrowed and his lips drawn back in a grimace that revealed his yellowing teeth (too much smoking already at his young age).

There were four in the car. Beside the driver I could see another face and through the open side window I heard him shout a loud "Yaaahooo!" I started sprinting as fast as I could, grateful that the sand was still moist and firm rather than the slippery powder above the high tide mark.

Beyond saving my life, I had a plan. I veered left. They veered left after me, getting closer by the second. I had no doubt they intended to run me down. Maybe that was not their intent, but I was taking no chances. I was certainly not thinking about turning the other cheek.

Things then happened in slow motion. I floated from step to step, feeling the car getting closer and closer. Knowing exactly what would come next, I sidestepped and, as the car began to pass me, I launched myself onto the running board on the left-hand side, the passenger side. The window was down. Now, with both feet firmly planted on the running board, with my left hand I grabbed the windowsill to hold myself steady. Like a striking snake, I delivered at least three very hard punches onto the jaw and ear of the guy in the passenger seat.

Next, as the driver swerved right in an attempt to throw me off, I leapt back to the ground and ran like a rabbit into the sand hills. After all, there were four of them in the car, and I'm not stupid. (Well, sometimes). I had a head start so before they had time to stop, tumble out of the car and start after me, I was over two big sand hills, and lying motionless and out of sight in some tall pampas grass (known as toetoe in New Zealand).

To be honest, my beating heart was somewhere between my chest and my mouth. There was no way I could take on all four at once (that would come in another time, one at a time). Fortunately, as they breasted the sand-hill above me, but unable to see me in my hiding place, one of them shouted, "He's gone," at which they gave up.

The sound of their departing V8 was music to my ears. Bullies will be bullies. But I figured my father would have been proud of the way I handled those guys.

Chapter 20

Love With A Belt

AS WITH MANY FAMILIES, my relationships with my parents and my brothers and sister have been off again on again over the years.

Nevertheless, past times bring back many memories, some of the best and a few best forgotten. And then there are those in between, those that are seldom recalled but which are not entirely lost, even though they are a bit foggy around the edges.

I have many memories of my father, and this one is well worth recounting.

It involves Byron as well.

About four houses down the street from us lived the Sandbrook family. Winston and Nelson were the oldest boys, Nelson being the oldest of all of us.

Byron became friends with Winston. I really did not - probably because of an emotion that was new to me, but it would pop up any time Byron and Winston got together. Now I can say it was jealousy, but then it was just a fact that I didn't like Winston much, and until the night in question, I had virtually nothing to do with Nelson.

What happened was that Nelson was old enough to leave home. He found a job somewhere locally, and accommodation in a single room at a cut rate in the one hotel in town. He had moved almost a full mile from home.

As we often did, Byron and I had walked that mile to town on a Friday evening. We hung out till the shops were closing. It was time to go home, so we headed past the hotel. Nelson appeared from the opposite direction. Under his arm, he was carrying a big brown paper bag.

"G'day" said Byron. "G'day" was Nelson's response.

"Watchya got?" asked Byron.

"Beer. A bloody flagon."

"Okay. See ya."

"Nah! Come an' ava drink, will ya?"

Byron paused, cast a sideways glance in my direction, then addressed Nelson again.

"What about 'im?"

Nelson paused for at least half a minute to think it over.

"Ah.... or'ight then."

At the time, the legal age for drinking was 21. Nelson must have been that age, else he could never have bought a one-gallon flagon of draught beer.

For my part, the thought of having a beer reminded me that Pete Clapham had introduced me to shandies, Portigafs and beer long ago, but I had never been in the habit of telling the family. This was prudent because my mother was of the opinion that beer was the undoing of many a man, and could even be sinful in the eyes of the Lord. That did make me wonder why he had turned water into wine, but I thought better of trying to score a point when she smelled the beer on my breath when I got home.

Wrigley's chewing gum was the answer to that thereafter.

Once in his room, Nelson pulled a stolen beer glass from his cabinet, opened the flagon, poured a beer, and downed it nonstop.

Byron was next.

My turn came. Half a glass was all I got. Right then I decided I liked Nelson even less than Winston, especially because they were both grinning that supercilious big brother, big boy grin that will tick off any younger brother in the world.

By the time the flagon was empty, Byron was as happy as can be. This was the Byron who could pick up and play any instrument you could think of, and sing as well. He would eventually have his own band and be billed as "New Zealand's Elvis Presley."

As for me, I was, according to my mother, tone deaf. Apparently she got that right - or I got it wrong and refused to take singing lessons. Perhaps she should have done that herself. Her high-pitched voice in church was truly distinctive. I noticed certain women in the choir casting quizzical frowns in her direction. Wondering why, I listened more carefully, and I seemed to notice that her voice was just a shade off key. But what do I know?

I do know she didn't like the smell of beer, so to arrive home after this three-man miniature party smelling of the devil's brew would be a life-ending thing.

Byron didn't seem to care. He sang all the way home, totally ignoring me as we got close to the house, still singing drunkenly at the top of his voice.

As we stumbled up the stairs into the front porch, Mrs Eagle Ears was there in a flash. The singing stopped. The shouting began.

"Hec," she shouted (that being our father's name) "these boys have been drinking!"

Dad appeared from somewhere.

"Drinking, eh?"

"Yes. Drinking. They smell to high heaven."

"I'll talk to them in the morning."

"No you won't. You'll give them the strap right now."

"I will? Because they had a couple of beers?"

"Yes you will. Take them into the bedroom and give them six of the best." She paused, then added, "Each."

Byron had to have his say.

"Nah Mum. S'alright. We jus' hadda liddle bid."

Aware that she was about to go ballistic, Dad started unbuckling his leather belt and said "C'mon boys. Into the bedroom."

Once inside, he closed the door, looked at us as we backed against the wall alongside our beds, one standing like a wobbly sheep (Byron) and a defiant little git (me).

Running the belt through his left hand, he sort of smiled and gave us some very surprising instructions, starting with a solid THWAK as the belt laid into the wooden foot-board of Byron's bed.

"Okay,," he instructed. "Yell like you've been hit."

Byron wasn't so drunk that he didn't get the message, while I suddenly felt a real sense of understanding about what the Old Man had to put up with, and even admiration for what he was doing right now. And so it went, 12 times, with Byron yelping for the first six, and me, almost doubled over to try and stop laughing, taking and faking the pain of the next six.

As soon as he had completed whipping the bed, and in his loudest Dad voice, clearly for mother's benefit, he all but shouted, "Now don't do that ever again." Then, he reached into his shirt pocket, handed each of us a piece of gum, and said, "Spearmint is the best. Juicy Fruit is no good at all." Saying that, he left the room.

Byron looked at me and whispered in a slurred voice, "I think he loves me."

As unfamiliar as I was with the concept, let alone the word, I retorted, "What? Go to bed!"

I did too, but my feelings were not exactly those of a well-loved child. I reached for the slug gun under the bed, pumped it, primed it with a slug, and shot the plaster cast of Danny Craven right between the eyes.

Confession:- I made up that last bit about Byron's love quote and the gum. It was actually me who thought for a fleeting moment that Dad actually did love us, in his own non-verbal way, although the shooting of Dany Craven did happen on another occasion. But hey, memories always get embellished, don't they? Or, as a Radio New Zealand copy editor would tell me 20 years later, "Never let the facts spoil a good story." And that virus, as it were, would eventually permeate all the world's news media - and give me reason to quit the mainstream news business completely to go my own way with no strings attached.

Chapter 21

Work Comes Easy

I N THOSE DAYS, AND even before we were into our teen years, finding work was never a problem.

First, the paper run, then as I got older and stronger, school holidays would see us working on local farms. This might be cutting thistles or hoeing and thinning a crop of mangolds - a type of fodder beet grown to feed out during the winter months.

Picking up spuds was the worst. I lasted only a few hours dragging a sack that got heavier by the minute as I filled it with freshly unearthed potatoes, which farmers grew by the acre for the local market. My hips and lower back could not handle dragging what became a 50-pound dead weight, so I reluctantly quit without pay.

As far as mangolds were concerned, they were an early summer money-maker for six seasons. I started working in a small gang when I was 12 years old. Planted in rows in lots of about five acres, they had to be thinned to nine inches apart in order to reach optimum size for harvesting and feeding out next winter.

Our six-week summer break from school would begin at the end of November, and I personally could not wait to get out in the fields. Daylight and the rising sun at that time of year would sneak out of the east around 4am, and with it would come the sound of Pete Clapham's old Essex car pulling up outside our gate.

Pete had been in the Air Force as an armorer with my father. They had both been overseas during the Pacific campaign in World War Two. I recall my father saying it would take a crew of four to service and arm a plane during training at the Ohakea base in New Zealand.

Overseas and under the constant threat of attack by the Japanese, they cut that down to a 20-minute turnaround. The only exception was if they had to replace a burnt-out machine-gun which a rookie pilot might have over-heated and destroyed by firing all his ammo at once, rather than in five-second bursts.

Pete could turn his hand to anything, as could my father, when it came to earning for his family. Pete had his own small herd of cows, drove a combine harvester every season to thresh and bag wheat, peas, and barley, and employed boys like me for his annual mangold thinning contracts.

Sometimes he also took me into a country pub after a hot day's work. There, he bought me a shandy - a mixture of beer and lemonade - or a Portigaf, which I remember as being port and raspberry cordial. Considering there were six of us kids in my family, that was a lot of mouths to feed. No surprise then that my father had us out working and bringing in a few shillings and pence each week as soon as we were old enough to use a hoe.

It was always a pleasure to hear the sound of Pete's old car arriving at our place at 4.30 in the morning. His idea of daylight saving was that we should start as early as possible, do at least eight hours, and quit before the summer heat got too intense. I would grab a sandwich made the night before, then jump in the back and doze off for the 20-minute drive out to the job.

On one occasion, I went sound asleep in the back seat, oblivious to the fact that everybody else was quickly out of the car, sharpening their hoes, and ready to take on the day. On those mornings, Pete would roughly shake me awake, snapping at me to get on the job, saying words that only a rough and uncouth man would use. I stored them away for later use when I too would become a somewhat rough and uncouth man myself.

There's much to be said for a day in the fields wearing but a pair of shorts, the soles of your bare feet, released from the strictures of your school shoes or sandals, toughening up in the cool dry dirt. With the sun beating down, turning my part-Maori skin to suntanned perfection, I would shuffle down one row and back up the next. By the end of the day, I would have carefully and meticulously thinned a full mile of mangolds. (It was only after I moved to America in 1990 that the full consequence of all that exposure to the sun would be revealed. I developed melanoma skin cancer.)

Home. Sleep. Do it again tomorrow. But go to Sunday School, Bible Class or church on Sundays.

We were paid according to the distance we had covered in a day. Distance was measured by the chain, a chain being about 22 yards in length. Rows were usually five chains long, and 80 chains were equal to a mile. The money of the time in New Zealand was in pounds, shillings, and pence. We were paid nine pence per chain, which added up to a tidy sum by the end of a week. In fact, on a good week I made a few quid more than my father, and in one six-week season (I think it was maybe 1959/60) I was able to buy my first motorbike - a 250cc BSA C10 side-valve which Byron later crashed and bent out of shape and beyond repair.

Some of what I earned from the mangolds and didn't spend on a transistor radio to hang on my belt as I worked, or a set of throwing knives or pellets for our slug gun, would go into the family coffers. Or some would be used to buy Christmas presents, such as an expensive full set of 33rpm vinyl records for my mother.

Although we were years away from the wonders of black and white television, we had a combination radio/record player with rather good speakers for the time. On that Christmas day, the house was filled with the sound of somebody's tabernacle choir singing the Hallelujah Chorus.

My mother was very pleased.

I, however, would secretly wonder what it would be like to be God and have to listen to that choir singing the same chorus in heaven for eternity.

Chapter 22

Top Of The School

G OING BACK TO MY time at Lytton Street school, there's not much more to say, except that much to my surprise I left as one of two who topped the school.

I had made friends with Alistair Williams, whose parents had migrated from England. They spoke funny, which my mother said was because they had been "upper class." I got along fine with Alistair, but I didn't think much of his sister Jan, who knew nothing about boys' games. He also had a younger brother, Simon, who was too young to play with, anyway.

The headmaster and Mr Williams spent quite a bit of time socializing together. They would attend cricket and rugby matches at the school, and I now grock the fact that this had a lot to do with Alistair being selected by the headmaster for the ultimate reward - he would be named as the school's top student at graduation.

In America, students who do well graduate as what's known as magna cum laude, summa cum laude, or just cum laude.

In Commonwealth countries, the term Dux is used for "The top academic student in a school, or in a year of school."

One day, I noticed Mr Goodwin and the headmaster talking outside during a morning break. Judging by Mr Goodwin's jutting jaw, the conversation was rather serious.

What followed a week or so later really did catch me by surprise. The headmaster announced that this year, two students would share the top honors; they would graduate as "co-Dux."

That was me and Alistair.

As a result, we were told we could now go to the local bookshop and purchase two or three books of our own choosing. I chose The Works of Shakespeare for one, 20,000 Leagues Under The Sea for another, and a fat dictionary.

I am sure one reason for selecting the Shakespeare volume was because my father had a way of saying "to thine own self be true and thou canst to no man be false." He was paraphrasing the lines from Shakespeare's Hamlet, "This above all: to thine own self be true, and it must follow, as the night the day, thou canst not then be false to any man."

I selected a dictionary because I had found that if I came across a word I did not fully comprehend, I would lose the plot in whatever I was reading. The best way to remedy that was to look up the definition immediately, then sometimes check a thesaurus for synonyms and antonyms. Or I would open one or the other at random, just to surprise myself with an unfamiliar word I might use in my own writing efforts.

As a for instance, the word Zinjanthropus might pop off the page, to be defined as *"a fossil hominid, characterized by a very low brow and large molars."* My imagination would then kick into gear and I would drift off into wondering about the evolution of humanity and the absurd claim by so-called scientists that all life on this planet started when an amoeba in a swamp got smart enough to think about becoming a human.

How did that square with the Biblical story of Genesis, the creation of Adam and Eve, and that they had two sons and no daughters, and yet there were now billions of people of every ethnicity on Planet Earth?

We might get into that later.

My education at Lytton Street was over. It was time to hoe mangolds during the summer holidays, and start school next year at Feilding Agricultural High.

Chapter 23

School Shooting

A s ITS NAME SUGGESTS, Feilding Agricultural High School was, supposedly, primarily about teaching students the ins and outs of the farming way.

It was also what they called a "self governing" institution. This meant the older boys in the higher classes were responsible for discipline during break times.

We newbies were required to appoint a class captain, an honor that fell to my friend of the time, Tony Boyle.

Feilding Ag offered classes in math, English, social studies, music, chemistry and woodwork, all of which I attended in my short time there.

Track and cross-country running, along with cricket and Rugby were naturally part of the curriculum. Cross-country or distance running were my preferences.

I'm sure it has long since been discontinued, but we were all required to participate in "School Cadets." That involved regular training in military matters, including rifle marksmanship, for which the school had established an outdoor shooting range. Our instructors were either teachers who had been in the military during World War II, or real army personnel from the Linton Camp military base.

One of them impressed us immensely by demonstrating how a grenade with some sort of rod attached could be launched from a standard issue Lee Enfield .303 rifle. He went down on one knee, placed the rifle butt on the ground, inserted the rod into the barrel and angled the rifle roughly in the direction of the football goal posts. When he pulled the trigger that dummy grenade on the end of a stick, looking much like a skyrocket you'd shoot on July 4th (or Guy Fawkes Day in NZ) just flew through the air with the greatest of ease and right over the crossbar.

On the up side, I had already learned something about shooting with my father's single-shot bolt action .22. He and his brother, my Uncle Graham, had taught me all the safety rules and how to zero in on the target using the open sights. "Start below the target. Breathe out. Bring the barrel up, taking first pressure on the trigger. Squeeze as you see the bullseye."

I did as instructed, squeezed the trigger, and Uncle Graham congratulated me in a somewhat sarcastic tone. "Ummm!" he said, "A miss is as good as a mile."

Such praise, which it obviously was not, ensured that I became very well focused and could soon put bullets within a half inch of each other in the bullseye.

We also had a pump action slug gun at home, and I was rather adept at knocking birds off the power lines. The slugs traveled so slowly I could see them approach whatever bird I was aiming at. If it missed, I knew just how much to adjust for the next bird and the shot.

At school, I really liked the School Cadets days and our time on the range where we had to shoot at targets about 50 yards away. The rifles we first used were army issue Lee Enfield .303s re-barreled in .22 caliber and modified to shoot only one bullet at a time. This was done for safety reasons, and to eliminate the recoil of the .303 round. There is no recoil at all from a .22.

At the shooting mound we were instructed to lie down, shoulder our rifles in the prone position, and the instructor would shout, "Load! Steady! Aim! Fire!"

After some training with the .22s, we were issued real .303s. They kick like a mule if you don't hold the butt end hard against your shoulder. I doubt that the smallest boy in the group ever took up hunting. He was driven back at least three feet by the recoil of his first shot.

Our targets were set up between some tall trees where magpies would build their nests. Magpies are smart birds. They never quite got used to the shooting, but they did learn the routine. Loud squawks of condemnation and flapping wings would be heard as each volley was fired by the 10 boys below. The magpies would squawk angrily, lift off their branches, then fly perhaps 50 yards, circle and squawk some more, then return to their roosting.

After five shots and five forays by disgruntled magpies, we were allowed to inspect our targets. Mine looked pretty good, and then it was another five. "Load! Steady! Aim! Fire!"

As always, that was music to my ears, but suddenly, as I was working the bolt to eject a cartridge case and load the next bullet, we all heard a roaring command. "CEASE FIRE! RIFLES DOWN! ON YOUR FEET! ATTEN... SHUN!"

I cannot say who it was that shot that magpie out of the trees. It wasn't me.

But I do know that being subjected to what I saw as an unjust collective punishment, which involved holding our rifles over our heads and running around a quarter-mile track, really sucks.

Chapter 24

Bully For Me

To this day, I am dyslexic with a tape measure.

Although I have worked in carpentry and construction and even attended courses and written a book about building log houses in New Zealand, there's no denying the fact that when they say "measure twice, cut once," for me, too often, the cut is either half an inch too short, or too long.

Nevertheless, at Feilding Ag woodworking class was a pleasant break from sitting in a stuffy room listening to the English teacher, or the chemistry teacher in his smelly lab with its pipettes and vials and stinky stuff.

Our turn in the woodworking shop came right after the morning break. While the teachers were in the staff room drinking tea, we "self governing" kids would gather in the courtyard outside the shop, waiting for the instructor to come and open up.

Put a couple of dozen teenage boys in a situation like that, and at least one of them will want to be top dog. I forget his name, so I'll just refer to him as Top Dog.

He was a big, solid, strong boy for his age, but a bully at heart who enjoyed picking on younger and skinnier kids. Kids like me.

For several weeks, the scenario was always the same. He would walk around, rolling his shoulders, looking for someone to pick up and dump. His trick was to eyeball his next victim, say something like "your turn" and I'd watch them freeze in place like a cornered chicken. Top Dog would move in, trap their arms as he grabbed them in a bear hug, lift them off their feet, turn them sideways and slam them on the ground.

I studied his technique, certain that he would eventually have a go at me because I was rather thin and lanky at the time. I was perhaps a head taller than him because, as my father observed, I was growing like a weed. He was correct. When I was 14, I grew six inches in six months. I didn't stop until I topped out at 6 ft 1 inch.

The woodwork shop was built close to the school's perimeter fence, and quite a few of us would be leaning against it as we watched Top Dog do his thing.

On this particular day, dumping one kid wasn't enough for the bully boy. He bear-hugged a victim, pinned his arms, lifted him off his feet and smacked him down on the concrete path. Then he turned and looked at me.

I had been waiting for this moment. Stepping away from the post I was leaning on, I walked towards him, sneering, snorting and laughing all at once.

His face turned purple with rage as he charged, head down, arms spread wide, ready to embrace me with his one and only way of proving he was the big rooster among all these chickens.

Pretending to be scared, I backed away as he approached. Then, on contact, I raised my arms so he couldn't trap them. All he could do was wrap his arms around my waist.

Using my own variation of a bear hug, I locked my arms around his torso, locking my elbows into his armpits so he could not let go. Using our momentum to backpedal as fast as I could, I knew exactly where this was headed (pun intended).

By keeping him off balance, he was unable to complete his bear hug. He had no choice but to keep his legs moving. His arms were trapped around my waist, and his head was above my right hip.

When his head hit the concrete fence post, it was all over.

He slumped to the ground, looked up with glassy eyes, flushed beet-red at the raucous cackling of all the chickens, and never picked on anyone again.

Chapter 25

Bully For Bung

IN MY ERA, TEACHERS had the authority to discipline unruly boys with the strap or a cane.

The government has since outlawed the practice, and now wonders why gangs and crime are on the increase. Go figure!

Back then, we would get ix on the palm of the hand with a leather strap, and they really sting (but you say nothing), or six on the buttocks with a cane, and that really stings (but you say nothing).

I had a few of each in my time, occasionally justified and sometimes not. This time was not.

At Feilding Ag, we had a teacher whose nickname was "Bung."

Bung had a glass right eye.

I'm only guessing, but he may have lost it when he was in the infantry during World War Two. Several of my school teachers had been in the military, as had my father. Those who survived came home permanently changed. Nevertheless, they had to pick up the pieces of their lives. They took up all sorts of occupations in a small and beautiful country that had lost many of its best, fighting to rid the world of the scourge of the Nazis or the ambitions of the Japanese.

Little did they know that the wars they had fought in, including my grandfather in the First World War, were all planned in the late 1800s – a fact which I only became aware of in my later decades as an investigative reporter.

Although they would never confess it, many if not all of them suffered from shell shock, or what's known these days as PTSD - Post Traumatic Stress Disorder. Call it what you will, some of them, like my father, could never after watch a war movie without being excessively despondent and often very angry for days thereafter.

In Bung's case, his service had instilled in him a military mindset that brought to the classroom a well-honed parade-ground mentality. We were the raw recruits, and he was the ultimate sergeant major. Bung's real name was Mr Evans, but because of his glass right eye, he was always "Bung" to us boys. His brief moment in my life has been unforgettable.

He was our English teacher at Feilding Ag. His class was held between "morning tea" (for the staff) and the hour-long lunch break. My friend Tony Boyle and I had side-by-side desks at the back of the class. Tony was class captain, and he had chosen that spot so he could keep an eye on the rest of the class of about 30 kids, most of whom, like me, were about 13 years old. A motley and noisy crew, to put it mildly.

Instant silence would fill the room as Bung strode in, left eye taking us all in as he strode to his desk, faced us, reached down to his right, opened the top desk drawer without looking and withdrew a duster. "Quiet!" he would command, to a room that could hardly have been any quieter already.

Then, turning to his right with parade-ground precision, he would dust off whatever was written on the blackboard, and start over with the day's lesson.

On the day in question, what was written there was not to his liking at all. He walked in, turned left to look at us all, and was perhaps a little startled by the unusual silence and the grins and smiles on so many faces. Ignoring the occasional suppressed cough or choked-off giggle, he automatically reached down to his right and retrieved the duster from his top drawer. He then did that military about-turn to his right to face the blackboard, where he only needed one eye to take it all in.

We could all see the blood shooting up the back of his neck as he savagely wielded the duster to remove the offensive graffiti. All over the board in large white chalk letters was written "BUNG Bung, Bung Bung, Bung Bung Bung."

I turned to Tony at the desk beside me. As quietly as I could, I asked, "Why did you do that?" He had been the first into class. I had followed a few minutes later as he replaced the duster in Bung's drawer. Other students had started to crowd into the room as Tony and I took our seats at the back. Bung followed a few minutes later. And now, he was not amused. Not at all. "Seemed like a good idea at the time," Tony whispered back as Bung spun around to face us all.

"Who did this?" he demanded, staring down 30-odd boys whose eyes suddenly found something very interesting on their desktops.

I was not so smart. I just looked at him, taking in the apoplectic veins, rushing the blood through his neck to his head.

I certainly did not expect what came next.

The sergeant major snapped, "KNIGHT!"

"Sir?"

"Did you do this?"

"No Sir."

"Do you know who did?"

Of course I knew. But you don't rat on your friends, or as they say in New Zealand, you don't dob in your mates. But you can't tell a lie either. Therefore, being a smart 13-year-old, I answered truthfully, but evasively.

"I can't say Sir."

I waited for Tony to 'fess up.

He said nothing. Part of my brain started reevaluating our friendship. Another part had to continue dealing with this furious teacher.

"You can't say, or you won't say?" Bung snapped.

"Can't say Sir," I repeated.

"Right," came the next snarl. "Down to the staff room."

Oh shucks! That's where they take us to cane our butts at least six times, and with full force. Just to teach us to be respectful, obey, do as we're told, and respect authority no matter who is dishing out the punishment.

I am supposed to respect someone who is thrashing me? I don't even respect my parents when they do that, so what makes you think I'm going to respect a teacher who canes me for something I didn't do?

I said nothing. I took the lashing. And then the bell rang, and it was lunchtime. Time to quickly bike home, grab a sandwich and be back for Bung's next class.

Chapter 26

Revenge Is Sweet

WHOEVER DESIGNED AND BUILT our old house at 231 Kimbolton Road incorporated all the modern bells and whistles of that era.

It had no insulation, but it did have a good open fireplace with a wide enough chimney for me to be able to stand up inside - just because I could.

The cast iron tub in the bathroom was big enough to accommodate one adult or two children who needed to be scrubbed up at least once a week.

There was a laundry chute in the bathroom through which one's grubby clothes could be thrown into the semi-detached laundry for the weekly wash. In the laundry, washing water was heated in a big copper urn encased in concrete over a small fireplace at ground level.

Until we upgraded to a stand-alone electric washing machine with its attached ringer, it was a matter of boiling water in the copper, throwing in some grated soap, followed by the whites, to be stirred with a big round wooden stick. Coloreds came next, and that was my Saturday job - washing clothes for eight people.

Two concrete tubs were available for rinsing the clothes and putting them through a hand-operated wringer before pegging them to a long clothesline made of Number 8 wire that stretched between the laundry and the garage.

There was a narrow concrete path that ran from the back gate, alongside the one-car garage, past the laundry to the back door of the house.

(You need all this information because of what comes next).

Although I had not uttered a sound when Bung whacked my butt six times as hard as he could, I did not sit down on my bicycle seat all the way home. Instead, I remained upright, pedaling as hard and fast as I could while my mind was riddled with confusion.

I was at once confused about how Tony had done what he did, and why I had taken the beating that he should have had. Part of me felt like a little hero, but another part thought I had been stupid. Above all, I was outraged that Bung had singled me out for a punishment I knew in my heart I did not deserve.

In that frame of mind, I broadsided through the back gate and started up the path to the back door.

"Oh lookey!

A rat running across the path.

A rat running into the laundry.

Quick as a wink, I baled off my bike, ran into the laundry and watched the rat scuttle into the little fireplace underneath the copper.

Grabbing the long stirring stick from beside the copper, I slammed it into the fireplace, connected with my quarry, and it was game over for the rat.

I washed my hands of it, had a quick sandwich and headed back to Feilding Ag, determined to get there and be one of the first in class.

I checked the blackboard and noted there were still some scribbled words there from the morning session, but the word "Bung" was not among them.

That was a good thing, although Bung would - as he always did - grab his chalk duster and start all over again.

The room quickly filled with my classmates. Tony was at his desk beside me, but I wasn't talking to him at this time. I was more concerned about Bung, hoping he might have got over the morning's issues.

Apparently he had. He strode into the room, glanced at the blackboard, walked to his desk, faced the class, and with his right hand automatically reached down to get his duster from the top right drawer of his desk.

That was his blind side.

I watched, poker-faced, as he opened the drawer, reached in, seemed to freeze in place while even his glass eye took on a steely glint. He said but one word as he pulled the rat from the drawer and laid it on his desk.

"KNIGHT!"

"Yes Sir!

"That was me Sir!"

I take great pleasure in recalling that he was frothing at the mouth as he marched me off to the headmaster's office. There, I was berated by both and called a "little humbug" (whatever that was) before being told my time was up.

I was being expelled, never to return.

Home life got a little difficult after that.

Revenge does have a price, but in that case, and to this day, I consider it was a price worth paying.

Chapter 27

On George's Farm

I REALLY DIDN'T EXPECT it, but thanks to also being kicked out of home for six months, I learned a lot about farming.

Having been expelled from Feilding Ag, where I had learned nothing about agriculture, my parents were able to have me enrolled at Palmerston North Boys High School.

The law was that we had to attend school until we were at least 16, and if possible we should sit for the School Certificate which would somehow help us in our future chosen careers. I was counting down the days till I turned 16 from the first day I attended.

Boys High was some 10 miles by Madge Motors' old gray buses from Feilding. Quite a few boys and girls, who preferred not to attend Feilding Ag, traveled to "Palmy" boys' and girls' high schools throughout the week.

Madge buses had a full width back seat, behind which was the luggage compartment. I found a kindred spirit in Athol Simpson. The luggage area was not enclosed. Therefore, Athol and I could hop over the back of the back seat, hunker down out of sight of the driver, and light a smoke. I'm sure we were trying to impress the girls, and I am equally sure they were not impressed.

Before and after my expulsion from Feilding Ag, life on the home front had been a little difficult for a long while.

Exhausted most of the time by working several jobs and 18 hours a day, my father was anything but even-tempered. My mother was also constantly on edge, her tongue often just as sharp as the proverbial dagger. Although in later years my father and I would become good friends, there was a day, a Sunday at the midday dinner table, when I lost it, as the saying goes.

Sunday was the family's go to church day, or Sunday school or bible class, depending on our age. Having "given my life to Jesus" when I was much younger, for at least 13 weeks straight, I had prayed to Jesus to have my parents get their act together and stop fighting over Sunday dinnertime.

It didn't work. The arguing happened like clockwork, with my father on this particular day so angry and exasperated that he said something or threatened something that had me come to my mother's defense in a split second.

As the blood of anger flooded my head, I picked up the carving knife and headed for my father's throat. Two steps and I stopped in confusion. What the hell was I doing?

I stayed motionless, then I told them they should get divorced. Eventually, they did. But in the meantime, "for your own good" (a phrase my mother used every time she brought out the jug cord or had me select a thorn-studded whip from the Elaeagnus hedge), I was sent away for six months.

I wouldn't say they were really friends of hers, because my mother was not given to having friends, or perhaps other adults did not want to be friends with her, but she had known the twin brothers, George and Hughie Fraser, for decades.

Like all those of their generation, they had lived through the Great Depression and were therefore very frugal people. However, the twins had also won a major Australian lottery, tickets for which were available in New Zealand, and each had bought a farm.

George purchased about 100 acres close to Feilding and established a dairy farm with about 100 cows. Hughie meanwhile went the whole enchilada and bought 400 acres a little west of the Himatangi crossroads. He stocked it with hundreds of sheep, a lot of breeding cattle for the meat market, and a herd of horses.

I was first sent to live with George Fraser on his dairy farm.

He was a gruff, stubble-bearded, heavyweight man in his 50s. His wife spoke even less than he did. His two boys were cut from the same cloth. I doubt that the boys and I said more than 10 words to each other in all the months I was there.

Being gruff and speaking little does not a bad man make. To me, he was but another adult, a man to be wary of, while being willing to do what I was told, and to learn what I could under these circumstances.

You may find this a little shocking, but one of the first things he had me do was to shoot his dog.

He had dug a big enough grave in the backyard, then called on me to "come here," which I dutifully did. His old dog, a tan colored mongrel with hints of Labrador and Border Collie in his friendly demeanor, had been watching his master digging. Leaning against the fence was a .22 rifle.

Without another word, Mr Fraser handed me the gun, looked at his dog, and started to walk away.

The old dog struggled to its feet, tail wagging despite hip dysplasia, obviously making it a painful move, although he had never let that stop him in his daily task of slowly rounding up the cows and herding them in for milking.

As he moved to follow his master, always at his right heel, his master continued walking away, and without looking back at his friend, he said but one word.

"Stay."

Dutifully, the dog stopped. Beside the hole in the ground.

I did as I was told. I shot him in the head. I buried him with a heavy heart and a lump in my throat.

It was not my last mercy killing.

The school bus came by every morning at 8.30, before which I was required to rise at 4, round up the cows and help with the milking. It was winter, and I liked to sneak a cup of warm cream off the top of the open milk vat. Milking done by 7.30, I would chow down some lukewarm oatmeal porridge topped with cream and sugar.

Meanwhile, Mrs Fraser had made my two white bread and peanut butter sandwiches (which she did every day for six months) for school lunch.

Whatever the weather, rain, hail or shine, I had to be on the roadside ready for the bus by 8.25. My school uniform comprised a gray cotton shirt and thin gray wool sweater, black short pants, and gray socks above black shoes. My knees and exposed legs would turn red in a minute in those biting gale-force winds on a winter morning.

Once back from school by about 4 in the afternoon, it was time to round up the cows and milk them again. Then the evening meal, a lamb chop, mashed potatoes, and peas. Every night for six months.

After the evening meal, I would do my homework, or whatever self-appointed study I wanted to do. I created a chart on which I nominated a subject to study and memorize for each night of the week. My intention was to be at least in the top five the next time we had exams. Then it was off to bed at 11, and up again at 4.

Weekends were a little different, although the food was the same. I still had to be up at 4 to bring in the cows, but during the rest of the day Mr Fraser taught me how to use a shovel and iron bar to dig fence post holes. The bar was essential in order to loosen the ironstone substrate that was everywhere, just a foot or so below the surface.

I also learned how to string and fasten fencing wire - eight strands required, with wooden battens stapled between concrete posts set 10ft apart. Sturdy fences are essential, for cows and bulls really do believe the grass is greener on the other side and they'll never hesitate to put their weight against a fence as they lean over for another bite.

One day, finishing up a fence on my own, I learned that there's a right side and a wrong side to be on. We had set the posts and strung the eight strands of wire to divide a particular paddock in half. All that remained was to staple wooden battens between the concrete posts, a task which Hughie told me to do by myself.

One half of the divided field would be for his Jersey bull. Hughie had recently bought the bull, roped it to a post in the cow yard, then, like a rodeo cowboy, dropped it on its side, tied the rope off and inserted a ring through the bull's nostrils.

The purpose of the ring was to provide somewhere to attach a lead rope if ever that became necessary. The sound of the animal's bellowing haunts me to this day.

Hughie completed the operation without breaking a sweat, then shushed the animal down the race and into the field where I would be nailing up battens. "Don't worry about the bull," I was told. "That ring'll keep him quiet for a while."

The wrong side of a fence is when you're in a field where a Jersey bull is off in a far corner, shaking his head occasionally as he munches fresh green grass. If you know nothing about Jersey bulls, they have a totally different temperament than Jersey cows. I might have been able to walk up to Mr Goodwin's Daisy and milk her on the spot, but a Jersey bull is a very different animal. I know of two.

Having been assured by Hughie that there was nothing to worry about, and seeing the bull way off in a corner, I picked up my bucket of staples and hammer and walked to the fence where we had stacked a pile of wooden battens.

I had a few stapled on when, for some reason, the hair on the back of my neck stood up all by itself. Perhaps it was just instinct, but I automatically straightened up and turned around. There was the bull, a mere 20 feet away.

His head went down as he started pawing the ground, tossing his head and its dagger-like horns from side to side, the nose ring glinting in the sunlight while his cloven hooves were throwing up clods of grass and dirt as he started to charge.

As he did so, I grabbed an armful of wooden battens and threw them full force at his head.' That slowed him down for the two seconds it took me to vault the fence to safety.

Thereafter, I knew the difference between the right side and wrong side of a fence if there are any Jersey bulls around.

My second encounter occurred years later.

I visited a farm where my youngest brother, Roger, was employed to milk quite a big herd of cows. He and his girlfriend Suzie rode double on his horse from where he lived down the road to do the milking together.

It was that time of the month, which means any time at all for a bull who smells a cow in heat, and there were several such enticing females on this property.

I arrived just as Roger and Suzie were getting on their horse after finishing the evening milking. Parking my car on the roadside, I started walking down the driveway toward them.

Suzie was settling behind Roger when he shouted at me, "HEY! BEHIND YOU!," at which moment he dug in the spurs and the horse leapt forward while I spun around to see what he was talking about.

A sex-mad Jersey bull that had broken out of the neighbor's place was charging down the driveway, head down, and me as the target.

The nearest fence was my only hope of surviving. Two steps and a leap over a fence topped with barbed wire is a very sensible choice under such circumstances.

I hit the ground and rolled, safe from the bull, which was now turning tail and heading for home as "Rodeo Roger," Suzie, and the horse sent him packing.

I still have the scar on my left thigh where one of the barbs on the fence opened that muscle as I dived for my life.

(Roger would go on to take a national championship belt as the top heeling roper in the country in years to come. He always said Scotch had a lot to do with his success.)

Now, going back in time to my stint on George Fraser's farm.

I was really treated quite well despite the lack of conversation (and the peanut butter sandwiches for school lunch every day). Nevertheless, there were occasions when I felt like an outcast, a misfit, one who should only speak when spoken to.

Consequently, I experienced the occasional attack of what I came to know as the dark night of the soul. In such moments, those yet-to-be-answered questions would spin through my mind. Who am I, really? Where did I come from? What is love? What is the meaning of life? Why do people die?

That's how I discovered the comfort of being alone in a thunderstorm at night.

The storm reached its peak an hour or so after everyone else had gone to bed. I, instead, donned one of Mr. Fraser's old oilskin raincoats, an oilskin hat, and a pair of tatty gumboots. Walking out into the pelting rain, I reveled in the wildness of nature as I braced myself against gale-force winds, felt the sting of hard rain on my cheeks, and watched enthralled as lightning and thunder spoke to the distant mountains.

I was too young to understand that this was an omen - a portent of the storms I would endure and survive in years to come.

I have no regrets at all about that time and those events. And that was my life for six months.

It was now time for the August school holidays, which, by no coincidence, was also the peak of the lambing season.

Chapter 28

On Hughie's Farm

WHETHER THEY CONSULTED WITH my parents I do not know. I certainly hadn't heard from them. Therefore, I am surmising that the Fraser twins had had a chat concerning how busy the lambing time would be on Hughie's 400-acre property.

It was there that I learned how to pluck wool from dead sheep. And how to walk on water.

Hughie was, like his twin brother George, a dour and heavy-set middle-aged man. He smoked roll-yer-own tobacco, constantly, never removing a "fag" from his lips until it was burnt down to a soggy butt. That he would sequester in the left-hand pocket of his tatty old tweed coat.

At first I thought that was to avoid any risk of fire if he were to throw the butts away, which I noted was a bit more thoughtful than my habit of squashing them on the ground under my heel. Not that any adults knew I had the occasional smoke myself.

In truth, Hughie had his own reasons for pocketing the stubs. If he ran out of tobacco before his next trip to town for stores, he would reach into that pocket, crumble the dregs between his fingers, and roll a new one.

Hughie was never one to mince words. He would say a few, and that was it. I was instructed that I would be required to do as I was told, and I would be paid one pound, "a quid a day", he said, for my efforts.

I liked that. I had in mind that I wanted to buy a guitar, a six-string Antoria F-hole beauty. All I had to do to earn the 18 pounds it would cost would be to work for Hughie for three easy weeks. I would even have two quid left over. With no cows to milk twice a day, there would be no more getting up at four in the morning. Even so, I might have to be up at daylight, which would be no great hardship because August is midwinter in New Zealand, and the daylight hours are relatively short.

I was dreaming of a guitar and Easy Street, but the reality was that the lambing and calving season required constantly walking around that huge property, checking to see that no ewes had become cast. A cast ewe is one which has rolled onto its back and is unable to regain its feet. This happens during lambing because of their weight, their heavy fleece, and the extra burden of being pregnant.

I felt good about helping them recover, watching some of them stagger sideways as they struggled to get their balance, then trotted away to resume their ceaseless grazing.

I was also required to run down other ewes which were experiencing another sort of serious birthing difficulty. Instead of the lamb presenting its front legs and head and being progressively ejected like a slow-moving torpedo, a front leg had folded backward, causing the lamb to get stuck half in and half out.

Some ewes would do their best to give birth but eventually scramble to their feet and resume grazing, oblivious to the fact that unless attended to, the lamb would die, and they would follow.

Other farmers had trained dogs to grab and hold those ewes by the wool around the neck, so the shepherd could then approach and deal with the situation. For some reason, Hughie had no dogs. But he had me, and I did a good job. I could sprint, grab, and hold a ewe in a matter of seconds. Plus, I never barked even once.

Calves were also being dropped among his beef cattle herd. Most births were uneventful, so we'd find a newborn calf up on its feet, perhaps somewhat shaky but soon happily suckling at its mother's udder.

In separate fields from the sheep, the cows and steers had many acres to roam over, including a swamp patch. These animals were semi-wild, therefore Hughie seldom got off his tractor when he was checking them out. Maybe that was because he had me to do all the footwork among the sheep while he sat on the tractor rolling smokes? That's a joke. He did insist that I sit up on the mudguard (fender) above the right rear wheel. This turned out to be a very good place to be.

Two incidents are worth recalling. First, as we drove through one of the biggest fields, his monster Black Angus breeding bull seemed to appear out of nowhere. He charged the tractor on my side, slamming into the tire beneath me before backing off and trotting away, his tail in the air signaling that he believed he had won the battle.

Further on, an angry cow stormed out of a swampy hollow. She had given birth very recently. Her calf was lying in some thick mud, unable to get to its feet. Left in that state, it would no doubt die. Surprisingly, Hughie drove as close as he could to the calf and stepped down from the tractor. Expecting him to be gored any second by the distraught cow, I was amazed to see him pick up the calf, hold it in his arms and face the snorting mother. She stepped forward, sniffed the calf, then backed away. Hughie then turned his back on her, which I thought was a very stupid thing to do. But no. He casually walked out to solid ground, the cow trotting behind him yet showing no sign of attacking him.

Turning again to face the cow, Hughie lowered the calf to the ground and stepped back.

The cow immediately moved up to the calf, lowered her head, and began licking the remains of the placenta off the calf's shoulder. Hughie stood and watched for a moment, casually climbed back on the tractor and we went on our way.

What I learned was that the mother instinct is extremely strong among (some) animals. I had yet to learn that it is not so strong in some of the human female species.

Spontaneous abortion at some stage of a pregnancy is one thing. There would have been seven siblings in our family had this not happened to our mother after she had already given birth to six of us. I know, because she called some of us into the bathroom one day. She was sitting in the bath. Between her calves there was a well-developed fetus curled up under the lightly bloodstained water. "This might have been your brother," she said.

Was that a spontaneous abortion? I don't know. But I do know that millions of women have aborted millions of babies since organizations such as Planned Parenthood were created. The founders of that institution included the father of Billionaire Bill Gates. They were into the science of eugenics – which means favoring one race over another, promoting abortion, and using a variety of other means to aid their depopulation agenda.

Now, back to the farm, and the saving of babies.

August also happens to be the rainy season, and in that year, the rain persisted for so long that two of the local rivers flooded.

One of them, the Oroua River (the one I often spent time at many miles upstream at Feilding), ran through the middle of Hughie's property. It was bounded by high stop banks and there was a wooden bridge over it, across which Hughie was able to drive his diesel tractor and stock trailer to get to the bulk of his farm. But the other river, the Manawatu, perhaps three or four miles away, had no stop banks in that area, and the floodwaters from there soon began encroaching on Hughie's farm.

The rain refused to stop, and the Manawatu River continued to expand, putting his hundreds of sheep and young lambs in serious danger. The Oroua River was also raging, rising higher every minute and throwing debris against the wooden bridge.

Hughie roused me at 5 on a Friday morning, and it was a nonstop rescue operation from then till 5 on Sunday evening. That's 60 hours straight, with no rest for the not-so-wicked.

By torchlight at night and despite continual driving rain, we mustered sheep and lambs from paddock to paddock ahead of the incoming flood-waters. Separated from their mothers, panic-stricken in those circumstances, the lambs were impossible to drive through the various gates to safety. Therefore, it was a matter of getting them bunched in a corner, grabbing them one by one, and throwing them into the stock trailer so they could be transported to the stop-banks. There, they would be left to their own devices to reconnect with their mothers. And, surprisingly, over time, all but a few mothered up successfully.

People might say sheep are stupid, but I was impressed by the mystery of how a ewe and lamb could find each other, even though hundreds of lambs and sheep were all bleating at the same time. It spoke to me of an intelligence that was beyond my comprehension; a miracle of Nature, a double miracle in some cases, because many of the sheep had twin lambs and they too reconnected correctly.

As for those that had lost their mothers to the flood, we gathered them together, put them in the stock trailer, took them to the barn, and released them there for shelter. Later, I would be tasked with bottle feeding them for a day or two, and they would again be released into a field of their own.

By Sunday evening, we had done all we could to save as many as we could from the rising water.

Ewes and lambs had been our first priority.

The cows and steers made their own way to relative safety, and we had opened the gate to the horse pasture so they could find higher ground themselves. Strangely, though, they bunched together in a corner of their field where the rising water was eventually up to their bellies.

They had been there for 24 hours while we dealt with the sheep and lamb rescue operation. With that mostly under control, Hughie drove his diesel tractor into the horse field where he was able to convince about 20 horses to leave the waist-deep water and straggle out of the open gate toward the nearby flood-bank.

Believing the horses to now be able to graze on the grass along the flood-banks, Hughie did not stop to close the gate. He continued driving past the horses, all of which turned as one and ran back into the belly-deep water.

We left them there. They all survived.

Chapter 29

Walking On Water

H AVING WORKED 60 HOURS straight till 5 on Sunday evening, Hughie had said it was time to quit. I was in bed in a minute and slept till 9 the next morning. The sun was finally breaking through and Hughie had already reconnoitered the situation outside. He woke me with one harsh word. "Giddup."

Very soon I was on the trailer behind the tractor as he drove toward the wooden bridge over the Oroua River. Confined by its flood-banks, the river was still in a raging fury. The bridge was dancing side to side, pummeled mercilessly by a massive logjam of trees and branches that the river had scooped up in its downstream run. It looked as if the bridge was ready to go downstream as well. Much more of this and it would be on its way.

Hughie turned off the track, spun the wheel a few times, and expertly backed up to the stop-bank.

"Grab the rope," Hughie said.

There it was. A long rope that he had tossed into the trailer.

Tying one end of the rope to the back of the trailer, he paid it out as he said "C'mon," and led the way to the top of the stop-bank.

"See that key log?" he asked, pointing to something about 40 feet away in the middle of the river. It was a long old uprooted tree around which everything else had gathered, got stuck, and over time had created a 20-foot-wide dam of driftwood up against the piles of the bridge, stretching the entire width of the river.

"Tie it around that," he said, "and I'll pull it out with the tractor."

Even for me, it's almost impossible to believe what I did next.

All he was asking was that I should run or skip my way across that huge floating logjam and tie a rope around the branch of a tree.

To use a common Kiwi phrase that usually follows a dumb move, it seemed like a good idea at the time.

Saying nothing, I grabbed the end of the rope and sprinted across the crazily undulating dam to that key log.

Quickly looping it around and tying it off, then holding a branch of that tree to help my balance as the driftwood under my feet rose and fell, I judged what I had to do to get back to shore. I specifically looked for big pieces that would support my weight as I ran back to the bank.

I mean the bank where there was now no sign of Hughie. And then the rope went taught. Hughie was on the tractor, out of sight and on the move.

There's no way to really explain how I made it, except perhaps just another moment of divine intervention.

No horse ever came out of the gate faster. There was no time for fear; only an instant supercharge of adrenaline and wings on my feet. If I didn't reach the bank, I'd be dead.

And then, within 15 feet of the bank, the driftwood in front of me disappeared downstream, leaving an empty space, except for the rushing water, which I had to cross if I were to survive.

Still at top speed, I leapt as far as I could - but the distance was too great. My right foot came down and hit the water. And then my left. I expected to plunge and be gone.

But no!

I swear that the water compressed under my feet, just for a split second, and I bounded forward to the last remaining driftwood, from which I catapulted onto the riverbank.

I was safe and sound - but none too impressed with a bloke who almost cost me my life.

I topped the flood-bank as he stopped and turned in the tractor seat. He seemed surprised to see me.

"Good job," he grunted.

Once the floodwaters receded, some ewes and lambs that had been swept away could be found hanging in the fences. That was when Hughie handed me a burlap sack, took me down to the fence line, pointed across the ooze and muck left by the receding water, and said, "Go pluck those sheep."

By now, the storm was long gone, replaced by two days of warm spring sunshine, and by a zillion flies that had done what flies do to a dead animal. It was no simple thing to pluck the soggy wool from those carcasses.

I certainly wondered how a man could win enough money to buy a 400-acre property, stock it with hundreds of sheep, cattle and horses, and still feel the need to salvage dead wool because it was worth the money.

My other thought was that I was lucky to be alive because the day before I could have been dead.

To pay me as I left, Hughie pulled a huge wad of notes from an inside pocket of his threadbare jacket, counted off what he owed me, and said, "Here." That was it. No "thanks" or anything like that. Just "Here," as if he were parting with his left one.

My parents had come to pick me up. As I drifted off to sleep in the back seat, I had a surprising thought. Why had Hughie said "You're still here?" after that key-log miracle? Did he not want to pay me? I let it slide.

I had enough money in my pocket to buy that Antoria guitar, and it was time to go back home, and the last term at Boys High.

Chapter 30

A Greenstone Jewel

MY PATERNAL GRANDFATHER, GRANDDAD Knight, had established a watch and clock repair business in Palmerston North. Sometimes I would deliberately miss the after-school bus back to Feilding and go and visit him for a while before catching a later bus home.

Like my father, Granddad was a man of few words. He was focused on his trade as a jeweler, just as my father focused on his as a bootmaker.

Both had their workbenches and tools of their trade within hand's reach.

For a time, before opening his own shop in Feilding, Dad had set up a boot-last anvil on a bench in the detached laundry. A "last" in this case was a solid iron base above which he could interchange various sizes of iron facsimile feet on which to work the leather shoes he was so adept at. His tools littered the bench, or were on shelves where he also stored old tins and bottles.

Guess who discovered there was ammunition in a tin up there? One of them was at least four times bigger than a .22 bullet. (It was a .45 slug, as used in the Webley .45 by the British and Commonwealth military).

The iron base of the last was secured to the bench with only three bolts. The fourth held some promise for an inquisitive kid. The hole went right through the bench.

It was the perfect diameter in which to fit a .45 calibre bullet.

That part of the scheming kid's dumb act of the day completed, the scheming kid grabbed a hammer and nail punch, and hit the .45 really hard.

The noise was deafening. The hole in front of his right foot toes was also a bit of an education.

The kid was very glad his parents weren't home that day. He was careful to remove the bullet case from the last, but retained a hankering to own his own Webley, one of these days.

On my visits to Granddad's shop, he would sit me down at his backroom workbench and let me fiddle with watch springs and some of the small polished stones from which he was adept at making necklaces.

One day, he offered me a small piece of greenstone, already shaped and polished like a miniature sword, perhaps two inches long.

"See what you can make of that," he said. "There's this too," he added, handing me a shiny gold chain

Greenstone is a hard granite-like volcanic rock that has been used throughout the world for thousands of years to make tools, statues and even weapons. One of those weapons, well favored by the Maori tribes of old, was a hand-held flattish paddle-shaped club known as a mere (pronounced me [as in bet] - re [as in re.]).

Held in the hand with a thong through a hole in the tip of the handle and looped around the wrist, it was as lethal as an iron tomahawk or hatchet. Some warriors became skilled at driving the weapon sideways into an opponent's temple, cracking the top of the skull, then twisting the mere to complete the death blow.

However, those who took heads and dried them as trophies were probably a little more careful in dispatching their prey. This would have been particularly true when the British arrived with their muskets.

I do not know whether it was the British or the Maori who started the trade, but I have images of many preserved Maori heads hanging like trophies on a wall. In wars between the tribes, either side could wind up with captured enemy combatants who would become slaves to the victors. Their eventual demise might have been the result of cannibalism, or because their preserved heads could be tattooed and traded for muskets.

Whatever the truth of that, early British officials took the heads back to Britain. There they would be exhibited in a museum display about the ever-expanding empire on which the sun never set. That's a correct statement too, because the empire stretched from the far north to the far south of the planet. Spanning many time zones and datelines and latitudes and longitudes, the sun was always shining on one of their conquered realms somewhere.

Under Granddad Knight's sideways watching gaze, I crafted that sliver of greenstone into a necklace on a gold chain. I did such a good job that I just knew it would fetch a good price when added to his array of handmade jewelry locked in the glass display cabinet on the counter up front.

As I handed the finished piece of jewelry to him, he smiled, just a little, and said, "That's good work. Your first piece. Consider it yours, my boy. Perhaps you'll join the business one day."

Not revealing my own thoughts about spending a lifetime in a back room at a workbench, I stuttered my thanks, pocketed the necklace, took it home, and hid it in a sock way back in the corner under my bed.

Speaking of greenstone, many years later, while exploring the "spiritual realms" such as purported psychic abilities, I attended a talk by a Maori man who showed us a greenstone mere. It had been discovered during an archaeological dig at an ancient village site somewhere in the South Island. Quite skeptically, I listened as he told us how a piece of rock could "speak" about its history, and how some people could enter a trance and "see" the ghosts of people who had died, or look into the past, and even the future.

He claimed that certain Maori individuals had always had that skill. They were known as the Tohunga - not chieftains, but men (and sometimes women) with unusual psychic abilities. He said all things have an aura, including people. It varies according to the individual's mood and temperament.

He caught my eye while saying that, but if I had an aura at all, it definitely had its dimmer switch turned down. I could see nothing anywhere, not about myself or anyone else in the room. I filed the thought of auras and what they might be into the weird stuff basket and got on with life.

Chapter 31

The Algebra Mystery

WHEN I TRANSFERRED TO Boys High after being expelled from Feilding Ag, I found myself in a mathematics class taught by a recent graduate from Teachers College. That means he was in his early 20s and destined to teach the same subject every day for the next 30 or 40 years.

I already knew arithmetic, however algebra was something new. I also had a short-term photographic memory. It was really handy in classes where I could instantly recall whatever the teacher wrote on the blackboard, then erased, and asked us questions about.

My first algebra class took things to a new level. After jabbering for a while at the 25 or 30 of us who were just starting the algebra journey, the teacher wrote some incomplete algebra symbols on the blackboard.

He then spoke some gibberish about solving this to get that. While I knew very well what 2+2=4 looked like, and how to add, subtract, divide and multiply, the squiggles and random letters he came up with might as well have been what passes for cursive writing in China.

As he chalked the answer on the board, he said, "There. See. It's simple." Simple to him maybe, but I was flummoxed. Next, I watched his every move, trying my best to figure it out as he scratched some more weird things on the board. Turning to face the class, he asked, in a demanding way, "Who can solve this equation?"

By the tone of his voice, it was obvious he did not expect any of these new boys to get it right. He had probably been trained to use this technique to exert his authority. If so, he needed to pick someone who could cement his position as the class boss. Perhaps because I looked confused, he pointed to me and said, "Knight?"

I might have been confused, yet I was also extremely focused. Hearing my name called, I briefly closed my eyes, visualized the board, and gave him the answer. It was correct.

Looking very surprised, he said nothing, turned to the board and wrote another unfinished thing in algebra. He then called on me again, and again I closed my eyes briefly, and answered correctly.

"How did you do that?" he asked, a note of disbelief in his voice.

"I don't know," I responded, honestly.

To this day, I recall that guy as a total dork.

He lost it.

"Get down to the staff room," he said. "I'll teach you not to fool with me."

Oh shucks! The staff room! That means the cane. Again. Six of the best, at least.

As he stormed out of the room, I started down the aisle from my desk at the back. The boys on either side of the aisle responded with a well practiced routine, a countermeasure if you will. Three or four of them handed me their school caps, and by the time I reached the door, they were down the back of my pants.

Even without the protection of the caps, I had found over the years that the strap or six of the best really doesn't hurt a bit. All you have to do is close your mind off and refuse to feel any pain. But what does hurt is being caned for telling the truth.

Frankly, that experience was very much like déjà vu. The caning was topped off by being marched into the headmaster's office. ("Have I been here before? Is this an expelling offense?") I wasn't expelled, but telling the truth didn't work either.

The headmaster asked how I had come up with those answers, and again I said I honestly did not know. He then sent me back to class, saying I must respect my teacher in the future.

That future never eventuated. I did not go back to his classes. Instead, when leaving Feilding on days when they were scheduled, I would have the bus driver let me off at the bridge over the Oroua River.

I spent a lot of time down at the river, so I learned nothing about algebra, but I learned about the birds and the bees - the real ones.

The sound and sight of honey bees gathering pollen for their hives was far more enjoyable than listening to a teacher in a stuffy classroom. Watching seed pods explode and send their contents flying in all directions often got me pondering the cycles of life. How had God made all this in seven days? I wondered.

I also learned from my quarterly report card that I held a record for truancy - 80 half days in one 12-week term.

When it came to sitting for the School Certificate, I did not pass. My major failing was in mathematics. In some of the others, I scored up in the 90s, but for math, I sat in the test with no intention of answering the various questions correctly. I did not know most of the answers, anyway. Therefore, when the results were handed out, I had scored two for math - and you get one point for sitting the exam.

Now, I can say there were two reasons behind that dismal score. First, it was because of my abhorrence of unjustified punishment. I rebelled and played hookey to the max. Second, I allowed my emotions (anger in that case) to over-ride common sense. Therefore, I chose not to learn a subject that could well have been of real value in later life.

Similarly, I also scored poorly in French, because I did not believe a foreign language would ever be of any value, so I didn't study diligently at all. If only I had known I could have joined the French Foreign Legion, or become a waiter on a cruise liner, caring for all those gorgeous mademoiselles!

I wondered for many years how I had found instant answers to those algebra questions. I sensed it had something to do with the mind, whatever that was. Therefore, some of my pondering, down at the river, was about how does the brain work? Why don't my parents teach me about that? - to which the obvious answer was, "because they don't know either."

I did not realize that such secret questions would take me halfway around the world to learn that the brain is the gateway to the mind, which can pull gold out of the ethers.

Chapter 32

Half-brother - Runaway Father

THE CHRONOLOGY OF SOME things in life can get a bit skewed after 70-odd years. Dates no longer matter, although the memories are easily recalled.

Such is the case regarding what was inevitable - the separations, the getting back together, and the eventual breakup and divorce of our parents.

It's only because I've had similar experiences, and more than once, that I can look back and understand why it had to happen, and why it was such a drawn-out drama.

Suddenly, or so it seemed, home life had become somewhat peaceful. Our father had gone away. Having prayed for something like 13 weeks every Sunday morning for there to be peace at Sunday dinner, it never occurred to me that the fact that Dad had done a runner was indeed an answer to that prayer. There were no more arguments at Sunday dinnertime, simply because he was no longer there. Yep - answers to prayer are not always the way you demand or expect them to be.

To this day, I don't know why my mother suddenly missed the Old Man, except perhaps because he was (she claimed) being tardy in sending regular support. Or it might have been that she had to find work herself, which must have been hard for a woman whose only job experience had been at a telephone switchboard many years beforehand.

Whenever she found work, within two weeks she would tell me she could "no longer work for those people." Perhaps she quit, yet I have a feeling she was more often than not asked to leave. Politely no doubt, but being asked to leave sounds a lot like being fired.

Often, she would regale me into the wee small hours with her litany of woes and condemnations. One of her favorites was to claim I had a half brother over the hills in Woodville. Or was it Dannevirke? She was convinced that "he" (Dad or "your father," said in a tone that implied that I was much like him) had been unfaithful when she was pregnant with me.

Maybe it was true. She never got over it, and she never got over telling me about it. I couldn't figure out why she was so unhappy about a kid she'd never seen (if he existed) and why she was, at the same time, always unhappy with me?

It was a few days after the mangold season was over, sometime around Christmas or early January, that she asked Byron and me to go and find our father.

Where?

At the bottom of the South Island, we were told. Working in the freezing works at Invercargill. Invercargill is a thousand miles from the tip of the

North Island (Cape Reinga) and at least six or seven hundred miles from Feilding. Plus, we'd have to cross Cook Strait.

Why should we?

Because if we arrived unexpectedly, said our smooth-tongued mother, he would welcome us and he would want to come back and everything would be alright again.

We looked at each other, silently communicating our doubts and disbelief and hopes all in one, then, without saying a word, we went to our room, picked up our school satchels, and stuffed a change of clothing inside. We were ready to go on another adventure. But first, we need some backstory about previous adventures Byron and I had shared, and maybe a peek at my first experience of love.

Chapter 33

Plane Sailing

Having had some outdoor and survival instruction when we were in the Boys Brigade, hitchhiking to the bottom of the world didn't seem like such a daunting task at all because by now Byron and I were seasoned explorers.

One of our first adventures had been when we pitched a small tent and stayed overnight down at the river. It was our introduction to camping by ourselves. We scouted the river bank until we found a small hollow in which we expected to sleep comfortably. We slung a rope between trees, threw our calico canvas tarp over it, pegged down the four corners, and settled in for the night.

We certainly slept weel, until it rained and the hollow filled up with water.

On another occasion, we trekked together through the sand hills for what seemed like 10 miles from Foxton Beach to Himatangi, carrying small backpacks and simple survival gear to camp overnight.

We could have made the entire journey on the seashore, except that got boring after a few miles.

"I think we can save a few miles if we go that way," said Byron. He was pointing "that way" into the sand-hills. Being a good little brother, I followed the big brother.

It wasn't long before we found some goose eggs alongside a swampy pool. The one we retrieved from the remains of an old nest looked big enough to feed both of us.

Byron went about the hopeless task of trying to find dry twigs in the swamp, dreaming about making a quick small fire on which to fry the egg in the pan that was included in his military-surplus mess kit.

I quickly unsheathed my new favorite hunting knife, and cracked the egg open, only for both of us to realize that the stench of a rotten goose egg will have you running upwind in two seconds flat.

Our retching (I'm joking) was interrupted (I'm now serious) by the roar of a huge plane that seemed to come out of nowhere. It was so low we could see the pilot and co-pilot in the cockpit. We could also see the left wheel assembly dangling like a broken bird's leg.

It was a delta-winged Royal Air Force Vulcan bomber on a visit from Britain, now heading for the Ohakea airfield for a belly landing that could quite likely have it go up in flames, killing the entire crew.

We learned later that it had almost crashed as it attempted to land on the newly extended runway in Wellington - a runway that straddles a very narrow strip of land between Wellington Harbor and Cook Strait.

I have landed there often enough over the years to know the crosswinds can be so strong that planes sometimes need to approach almost sideways before the pilot flicks the controls to straighten up in that last moment of touchdown.

I have even been on incoming commercial flights where at the last minute the pilot has said, "This is the captain speaking. We regret that conditions at Wellington are too dangerous for a safe landing," and has then taken us to a safer place to touch down.

The Cook Strait end of the runway jutted well out into the sea. It had been extended because bigger domestic planes were being introduced, and they needed a longer distance for takeoffs and landings.

However, it was a very short distance and a very big challenge for a plane as big as the Vulcan. Too much of a challenge apparently, although the pilot must be commended for his quick reactions.

The wind caused the left wing to drop just enough on the approach that the undercarriage on that side was almost ripped out of its housing as it hit the drop-off on the Cook Strait end of the runway.

I guess it was a matter of slamming the throttle hard forward and pulling the stick hard back in order to get full throttle and save the day - and the plane and crew.

The only option thereafter was to fly as low and steady as he could up the coast. He was jettisoning fuel to lessen the chances of going up in flames as he flew over those two gawking boys in the swamp, and on to a belly landing at Ohakea.

He got that one right. They all survived.

Chapter 34

Two On A Tandem

WHEN FACED WITH A mechanical task such as tightening or loosening a nut and bolt, I have always had to start by reminding myself, "lefty loosey, righty tighty." It works every time, except on those stupid left-hand threads where the opposite is the case.

Byron had never had any such problems. He could just look at pieces of junk bicycle frames and, within a few days, turn them into a tandem bicycle. Naturally, I was required to be the co-pilot on the back seat as we gave it a test ride, all the way to Wanganui, which just happened to be 40 miles from home.

The trip took half a day, so it was fortunate that he had a shilling or two in his pocket and was able to find a red phone box, call home and say we'd be back tomorrow.

We spent the night in a band rotunda in the city park. A band rotunda is a roofed circular platform used by local brass bands or kilted bagpipe players during significant fairs and events.

Concrete does not an easy mattress make but a 40-mile ride on a tandem is enough to make a boy grateful to just lie down and doze off.

Came the morning, and Byron had a great idea. Why shouldn't we climb to the top of the 100 ft water tower over there? It would offer a spectacular view of the city.

No sooner said than done. We climbed to the upper platform, which was surrounded by a safety fence topped by a flat railing.

Recalling my expertise as a fence walker on the Christianson farm, I had a moment of fear, imagining that if I were up on that rail, it would be a very long drop to the ground. The twinge of fear was quickly replaced with the realization that the top rail was far wider than the one on those cow yards. This one was probably 4 inches wide.

It took me no time to clamber up there, hold my arms out like a seagull about to come in for a landing, and I walked right around the water tower.

Now it was time to head home.

At some point Byron muttered back to me, "these hills are a lot steeper than yesterday."

I said nothing, but feeling just a little guilty, I started pedaling properly instead of just allowing my legs to do nothing except ride weightlessly up and down as Byron did all the real work.

Byron took to mechanicing like a duck to water. Vehicles in those days required regular applications of grease to their various joints such as steering rods and drive shafts, and he was more than happy to service Dad's vehicles whenever needed. He could jack up a car, take off a wheel, grab some tire irons, and fix a puncture in no time at all.

He could take dings out of bodywork and repaint so well it would look like new. I know this because just after I got my license at 15, I was driving Dad's Bradford van at night in heavy rain with almost zero forward visibility.

What street lights there were, were few and far between and the pitiful wipers were about as much use as a chocolate teapot. Rounding a corner, I moved too far toward the curb, hit a parked car, and tore the left paneling of the van apart.

Byron was not amused at all, because he had just finished repairing it himself, having had his own unfortunate encounter with a power pole. While that might lead one to think that he crashed into a pole, the opposite is true. A power pole crashed into him. Yes, it did.

Byron was behind a truck hauling a pole on a trailer when, without signaling, the truck turned left. Byron veered right to get around the protruding pole, but it followed him in an arc that had it smash into the side of the van, turning the aluminum paneling into an early version of crumpled tinfoil. Understandably, having just completed that repair, he was less than amused with having to do it again after my crash on that dark and stormy night.

Chapter 35

Love At First Sight

E XPRESSIONS OF LOVE WERE never a big thing in our house - but when I first found what I took to be love at first sight, the feeling was just AMAZING!

Aside from long days in the mangold fields, I was still making time to go downtown on Friday nights, where I could hold hands with my first real girlfriend, Pat Wilson.

She was a well-developed 19-year-old. I was 15. Pat came home by train every Friday from her job as a nurse-aid at the facility for Downs Syndrome boys and girls down in the town of Levin, a small town between Feilding and the capital, Wellington, about 40 miles as the train flies from our family homes in Feilding.

I would meet her at the station, then we'd hold hands and stroll around town, checking out the trinkets in Woolworths and the very classy imported clothes in the store owned by the Eade family. One of the brothers, Mike Eade, had been my teacher in Bible Class in years gone by, and a very influential person in my decision to choose atheism over religion.

Knowing, as I did at 15, that we would spend the rest of our lives together as a happily married couple, I nevertheless knew it was too soon to buy a ring and get engaged. However, it was important to make my intentions clear.

One balmy Friday evening, I made sure the coast was clear, dived under my bed, swiped away the cobwebs, and retrieved my sock with the greenstone necklace I had hidden there many months ago.

She was quite speechless when I gave her that precious gift as we parted that night.

Putting it around her lovely neck, she then held up that very small piece of polished rock to let the streetlight dance upon it as she promised to cherish it forever.

She kissed me on the lips for the first time, and then I walked on air up the garden path.

Chapter 36

Follow Your Nose

T HE REASON I HAVE run with the theme of being a misfit is because although I have done my best to fit in to ordinary society, my questioning nature and the lack of adequate answers always made me feel out of place. Not in a bad way, though.

For example, my experiences within Christianity gave me a profound love for the teachings of Jesus. That love has endured throughout my life, despite my having temporarily taken the roads of agnosticism, then atheism, until finally, through yet another mystical experience, I found the answer to that burning question, "What or who is God?"

That was a question no-one in the Christian fraternity could answer except by saying "have faith," which is no answer at all. Nor could they specify where heaven and hell might be located.

To top it off, they never explained what Jesus meant when he said, "Know ye not that ye are Gods" (Psalm 82 verse 6 and John 10 verse 34.) or that, "The kingdom of God is within you." (Luke 17 verse 21). That has also been written as "The Kingdom of heaven is within you."

The only answers I was given were to the effect that Jesus didn't really mean what he said. He meant something else. It was just an allegory.

This apparently justified their many reinterpretations, explanations, and their perpetual retreat into dogma.

My journey into atheism began this way. Prior to being sent off to the Fraser dairy farm, I had been on my knees almost every night for thirteen straight weeks, praying that Jesus would stop them fighting.

Sundays were the worst.

It was mandatory for all of us kids to attend Sunday school or Bible class at the Feilding Baptist church. After that, we would have to sit through the minister's sermon before returning home for mid-day dinner, and argument after argument.

Gradually, over that three-month period, my childish trust in Jesus, God, his father, religion, and adults who purported to be Christians dissolved almost completely.

One incident comes to mind.

Sunday morning bible classes were divided by age and sex, boys in one room, girls in another. We were all required to bring our own bibles.

On one occasion, as we arrived at the church, my sister Marie said she had forgotten to bring hers.

I gave her the one I had and went into class.

All the other boys, about six or 10 of them, had theirs.

The teacher, Mr Mike Eade, determined what chapter and verse we should study. The other boys dutifully followed his instructions.

Then he said to me, "Where's your bible, Knight?'

"I haven't got one."

With that, he stood up, towered over me, took my nose between his thumb and forefinger, closed them like a vice, twisted sideways, kept his grip, pulled me off my chair and forced me to my knees.

"Don't you ever come to my class without a bible," he snarled, giving my nose an extra twist the other way.

Still holding my nose in that vice-like grip, he pulled me to my feet and propelled me back into my chair.

The pain made my eyes water, but I refused to utter a sound. Instead, I sat back and heard nothing he had to say, ever again. I just sat there, pondering this absolute injustice.

My feelings were a combination of resentment, anger and hate, with a bit of poor-me and victim thrown in.

It took me 25 years to get over it and finally forgive the man.

Until then, I considered him to be a hypocrite, a sadist, a bully, unfit to be teaching or preaching about the love of Jesus.

As he droned on after his unprovoked assault, I switched him off and started thinking for myself.

"Thinking for myself" is a very significant statement. I have been doing it ever since.

With him tuned out, the questions flooded in, as they would continue to do for many years. For convenience, most of them are listed here.

I had read the bible, and every chapter and many verses had raised questions.

Why did the God of the Old Testament tell people to kill their first-born? (Exodus 13 verse 15).

Who did Abel and Cain marry?

What about "the sons of God saw that they were fair, and they took wives for themselves of all that they chose." (Genesis 6 verse 2).

Who were "the sons of God?"

Where did the wives come from?

Who was Jesus, anyway?

Why was he the "only" son of God?

What about all those verses in Psalms that say we are all God's sons or children?

Why did they teach me that I was "born in sin"?

Why was I taught he "died for my sins" when, as far as I knew, I had committed none?

What about the millions and billions of people over the past 2000 years who had never heard of Jesus?

Where did they come from and where did they go after death?

What did Jesus mean when he said, "The kingdom of God is within you"? (Luke 17:21).

And, "Jesus answered, 'Is it not written in your law, I said, 'you are gods'"? (John 10 verse 34).

Why was I told Adam and Eve ate a forbidden fruit - an apple - when the fruit was not named in the bible?

How could a serpent talk to Eve?

Who wrote the bible in the first place?

If I had "given my life to Jesus" when I was seven, why was I now being taught that the devil would be after me for the rest of my life?

Why did our Baptist prayer book include the words "we who are lower than worms"?

What did Jesus do during all those missing years before he started his ministry?

How did he heal the blind man?

Those are just a few of the thoughts I have pondered, most of which have since been answered, at least to my satisfaction and understanding.

Mr Eade closed the class with a prayer we were supposed to say in unison.

I kept my mouth shut, and my questions to myself.

As usual, the following sermon in the church was all about what Jesus meant when he said whatever he said 2000 years ago.

Or it might have been time for communion which you could only participate in if you were 14 or older. We were expected to pretend we were at the last supper. Bread and wine, said the minister, represented the body and blood of Christ, and we were to drink of his blood and eat of his body and be grateful that he then went and died on the cross for my sins.

The very thought of it filled me with horror. "Cannibalism!" shouted my inner voice. I flat out refused.

I was on my way to becoming an atheist, while some of my siblings went through the baptism ceremony and have been devout, honest, topnotch examples of the best sort of christian throughout their lives - after a few "sins" and glitches here and there.

Chapter 37

Dad And The Big Freeze

MOTHER'S REQUEST, WHICH WAS more of a command, that we go and find our runaway father, was made on a Monday.

For personal reasons, I wanted to refuse, but I knew I couldn't. The reason was that I was head over heels in love with Pat Wilson, and she would be home on Friday. Suddenly, the light bulb flickered in my head. What if I went and found Dad, then came back on Friday, caught the train in Wellington, and then surprised her when she got on the train at Levin?

Great idea!

Mum fumbled in her purse, produced a few pound notes, and handed them to Byron. "This will help," she said.

I had made great money hoeing mangolds that season, and, for a change, instead of giving it all to Mum, I had stashed quite a bit for myself. No-one noticed that I slipped an extra sock into my satchel. It was my cash stash.

We caught the next train to Wellington, made the short walk to the ferry terminal, then the overnight trip down the east coast of the South Island to Lyttelton harbor.

We had paid the minimum fare, which gave us the cheapest bunks on the ship, right up at the bow, so we spent the night rising and falling as the ferry plowed through the ocean. My stomach did the same until at least an hour after my feet were back on land.

On the bus into Christchurch, Byron was smart enough to ask the driver for directions to the main highway south. "I can drop yer off right where ya need ter be," said the driver, and soon we were on the roadside, walking south but holding our hands out to thumb a lift as the few cars on the road went by.

After a couple of hours, we stopped for a sit down. As usual, Byron showed off his talent for recognizing the make and model of every car that approached and passed. Vauxhalls, a Bradford van, a Peugeot from France, a not-so-old Model A, a big 1938 four-door Chevy like Mum owned, and then one that almost had Byron drooling as it approached.

It was a blue four-seater Zephyr 6 convertible with the top down, and only the driver on board. Byron immediately stood up and started thumbing. The Zephyr pulled to a stop. The driver looked at us, asked "where ya goin'?"

"Invercargill" said Byron.

"Me too. Jump in."

By dusk we were in the southern-most city on the planet where we found a hotel, booked a room, spent the night, and figured out how to get out to the freezing works where Dad was supposedly working.

Byron said, "Let's get a taxi," and soon we were asking the man at the main office where our father might be. "Try the freezers," we were told.

Freezers are enormous rooms full of frozen and freezing sheep carcasses hanging from hooks and rails. We found our way past the many men doing their part on the chain at the end of which our father had the job of pulling the carcasses further along the rail and into the freezer.

Ignored by the chain gang, we made our way to the end of the chain and the doors to the freezer.

Once inside, we stood and watched. Dad had no idea we were there. His back was to us as he leaned into a row of hanging dead bodies, then pushed them like a collection of shopping carts far to the back.

He turned, saw us, his jaw almost dropped, and in a shocked tone he blurted out, "WHAT are YOU doing here?"

I left it to Byron, because I'd had the same thought myself. Why were we here? Life had been pretty good with Dad gone, hadn't it? Wasn't he better off without all the nagging and arguments and losing his temper sometimes with us - me in particular?

"Mum sent us," said Byron.

"Well, GO HOME" was the response.

That was it. There was nothing more to say.

We left and headed back to town, where we found a fish and chip shop and ordered the best fried oysters on the planet - fresh from the beds around the nearby Stewart Island. If God doesn't have those things in heaven, he's missing out on a lot.

Sucking on a mouth-watering morsel, I mumbled to Byron, "Hey, I think I'll catch a plane."

"What?!"

"I've got enough meself and you've got that money from Mum, so you don't have to hitchhike. You can catch a train back to Christchurch and get the ferry."

Byron was not amused, so it was pretty much a day of no-speaks, during which I found the booking office and bought a ticket for the first and probably only flight to Wellington the next day. Friday.

Chapter 38

Ain't Love Grand

I T WAS A FINE day and a fine flight. From the air, the Southern Alps looked amazing, some still mantled in snow, with Mt Cook towering above them all.

A bloke by the name of Ed Hillary climbed there often, and eventually became the first (so it is said) to climb the tallest mountain in the world, the 29,000 ft (and a few inches) Mt. Everest in the Himalayas.

After that, he became Sir Edmund Hillary and continued his outdoor adventures. In 1958, he headed a team using modified Massey-Ferguson tractors to cross Antarctica to the South Pole. This time, he wasn't the first to do so. Raoul Amundsen had started from somewhere else, and beat him by a month.

The landing at Wellington was smooth. A bus to the station got me there in time for the afternoon train north. It would make its way 400 miles in the next 24 hours to the bigger city of Auckland, stopping at every small town along the way, including Levin.

Love, it is said, is a many splendor'd thing, and I felt really splendid as the old steam engine huffed and puffed its way into Levin.

I had deliberately taken a seat in the last passenger carriage, knowing she would more than likely get on board a few cars ahead. Those wooden two-person bench seats either side of each carriage seldom saw a full house of passengers, so I was virtually alone, daydreaming my way north toward my future betrothed.

As the squeal of the brakes signaled we were coming to a stop at Levin, I peered expectantly through the window to see her on the platform. And there she was. She was talking to a guy dressed as a cop. They chatted until the old steam whistle screeched and the old conductor out there shouted, "ALL ABOARD!"

I watched, entranced by her beauty, as she smiled at the cop, hopped up the steps two cars ahead of mine. Soon the chug-a-chug-chug and billowing coal smoke and the sound of the whistle and spinning iron wheels getting a grip on the rails signaled we were under way.

My beating heart all but turned me inside out as I made my way forward, fully ready for that wonderful smile of welcome.

Pause.

I guess you've guessed it by now.

As I appeared and lowered myself into the empty space beside her, I was first greeted with anything but a smile.

It was certainly a look of surprise, but it was exactly the look and the way my father had reacted down there in Invercargill. "What are YOU doing here?" was NOT the response we had expected from him, and most certainly not what I had anticipated from her.

The trip hammer in my chest hammered harder. The blood rushed to my face. My vocal chords seized up. That infernal inner light-bulb went incandescent as I understood what I had never contemplated.

It was over.

She was dating that bloody cop in Levin and playing games with me in Feilding.

Suddenly, she didn't look so pretty after all. Her rose perfume that last week had my head spinning, this week was so strong it could've knocked a hummingbird unconscious in mid flight.

She had messed up her makeup, too. I could tell because her lipstick was all smudged.

What was that about? Yeah, I know. That cop again!

More to the point, what's that flashy ring doing on her left hand?

And where's the necklace with the greenstone gemstone?

Gone?

Yes. Gone forever.

The emotions of the moment were quite new to me. How can you feel love and anger and self-pity and jealousy and even rage all at the same time?

Not for another 30 years would I find the answer. And in the interim, journalism would teach me to ask the right questions, especially the quiet, private, difficult ones, about myself.

Chapter 39

The Manawatu Times

MY CAREER IN JOURNALISM really came about because I had had an aptitude for writing ever since I first put pencil to paper at school, or perhaps crayons to the wall at home.

Although I never understood nor mastered such things as nouns, pronouns, verbs, adverbs, or split infinitives, I could string words and sentences together in a way that always saw me in the top ten of any English exam that included an essay component.

I quit school the day I turned 16, having no academic qualifications, and no further desire to become a doctor. I had had that in mind since I was about 10 years old.

However, school was so utterly boring that the idea of spending another 10 years in university classrooms had eroded my dream of being a doctor. Instead, I decided to take my chances as a laborer, perhaps to become a farm boy.

It was my father who stymied that plan and set me on my path to becoming experienced in all types of news media over the next 30 years.

As one of the three jobs Dad worked to support his wife and six kids, he had a daily mail run delivering Post Office mail and newspapers for subscribers to The Manawatu Times. That was a morning newspaper headquartered in Palmerston North.

Somehow he convinced the editor to employ me as a copyholder, from which lowly station I might at some point work my way up the ladder of journalism.

Being a morning paper, the job required me to sit across a desk from the proofreader who, armed with the proof fresh off the Linotype, would read aloud, while I followed along on the reporter's original copy, only interrupting her if there were any missing words.

This we did from 6 pm till 2 am, which left me four hours to fill in before my father would arrive for his papers, pick me up as well, and I would doze off in his car until eventually arriving back home in Feilding.

During the four-hour wait, I would upgrade myself to being a pretend reporter in the now vacant newsroom. Inhaling the unforgettable smells of newsprint and stubbed out cigarettes in every ashtray, I would sit down and teach myself the art of two-finger typing at high speed.

The desk I favored most was assigned to Merv Dykes, one of the senior reporters, if not the Chief Reporter. He was good enough to welcome me to the newsroom when I first arrived. He made a point of suggesting that I use his desk and typewriter if I wanted to fill in time in the early hours.

That skill has stood me in good stead to this day. I can still type "the quick brown fox jumps over the lazy dog" faster than you can say "jackrabbit."

Then again, I still have to correct a lot of spelling mistakes too, especially since today's spellchecker technology misses a lot of typos.

Speaking of mistakes, some things that appear as mistakes are not. They are just life-changing incidents from which we can only see the benefit in hindsight.

The end of my time as a copy-holder is a personal case in point. That job lasted only six months, during which I tended to average no more than four hours of sleep a day. After arriving home from the all-night job, I would crash for a few hours and then be up and about until it was time to catch the bus and get back to the newspaper for another overnighter.

There came a weekend when my parents took some of us kids down to Wellington, close to 100 miles from Palmerston North. They knew I had to be back on the job by six on Sunday evening, but for some reason, they dropped me off on the highway just out of Wellington at three in the afternoon.

Three hours for one hundred miles should certainly have been enough for a hitchhike in those days.

However, there was a glitch. I was dressed in jeans and gumboots rather than the slacks and shiny shoes I usually wore to work.

It didn't take me long to realize that trying to thumb a ride while dressed like that was just not working. So I started walking. I kid you not, by 6 pm, which was my starting time on the newspaper, I was still 90 miles from my desk.

I had covered close to 10 miles on foot when I finally got a lift. It was a blessing, but almost immediately after explaining I was late for work and where it was, I fell asleep in the car. I finally woke up when the driver tapped me none too gently on the shoulder and said, "Oi, we're 'ere."

I was three hours late.

The strain of being both proof reader and copyholder in my absence had definitely taken its toll on the angry woman across the desk. Her temper got worse because despite my best efforts to stay awake, I kept falling asleep.

She would snap at me each time my eyes closed and my chin dropped to my chest. I would do my best to jerk myself awake, but eventually, the fat old lady lost her temper and shouted at me loud enough to raise the roof.

Without thinking, I responded with a word that shocked her to the core. I snapped a loud "EFF YOU!" (the real thing) and that was the end of that.

Trembling with anger, she wobbled her fat body to the editor's office, from which Mr Roche quickly emerged. Little flecks of spittle at the corners of his mouth indicated his depth of anger and disapproval.

This time I was not a "humbug." I was "an absolute ingrate," and I was out of a job. Fired.

It wouldn't be the last time either, but those few short months had cemented my ambition to become a reporter.

Being a starving author or one who might live from hand to mouth by selling articles here and there was not on my list.

I simply knew that writing was what I wanted to do, therefore to be paid for it as a journalist was the obvious choice. Yet having been fired from my first job in the trade, how would I ever achieve that ambition?

What should I do now that I was all grown up at 16, and out of work?

Chapter 40

Dust Yourself Off

R ECALLING MY FATHER'S OFT-REPEATED "I am the captain of my ship, the master of my destiny," I mentally brushed off the tongue-lashing I had received from Mr Roche, along with a relatively mild rebuke from my father.

It was now the end of summer, time for bringing in the sheaves - the real ones of wheat and barley and peas that farmers in the region grew every year to supplement their income from their sheep and cattle operations.

Pete Clapham was now driving an old but serviceable combine harvester. It was modern at that time, in the sense that it had replaced horse-drawn implements. Its job was to ingest the wheat or barley as it mowed its way around the field, threshing the grain (or berries) free from the stalks, spitting out the straw while the grain rushed its way through several tubes to be poured down one of four chutes into waiting burlap sacks.

Each would hold about 80 pounds of grain. They must be quickly sewn and thrown to the ground and replaced by an empty sack ready to be filled and sewn in its turn.

All that was needed was a worker who could keep up and keep busy, and that busybody was me.

On a good day I could sew, throw and replace 80 bags an hour, and that's not boasting. The boasting part is that I could also roll a cigarette with one hand in just a few seconds without losing time or slowing my sewing pace.

I was also making enough money to join Pete at the Cheltenham or Bunnythorpe pubs at the end of the day. Age 21 might have been the legal age at which one could go into a bar at the time, but Pete and the owners of those pubs seemed to think that leaving a 16-year-old out in a hot car in the parking lot was akin to cruel and unusual punishment.

I must admit that I fully shared that sentiment. The first drink Pete bought for me was a shandy, a mixture of cold beer and lemonade. It didn't taste too bad. He once suggested a Portigaf, which was a mix of port and raspberry juice, too sweet for my liking.

Although I was not at all talkative in the bar, I found that a cold 8-ounce beer and a cigarette had a way of improving my image of myself as a real man. (This worked for about two decades, thanks to a combination of beer and spirits and up to 60 cigarettes a day, although I did eventually quit both for about 17 years.)

As much as I enjoyed the hard work on the combine harvester, I also had to deal with knowing that I needed to find something to work at once the harvest was over. There had to be a better way to make money than spending eight or ten hours a day bouncing around on an iron seat. Not to mention the fact that it had no air conditioning.

Perhaps it was a godsend, because once we got into the barley, I had to quit at the end of the first day.

Barley dust was, for me, a total irritant. Like the finest glass dust, it turned my body into a raging itching furnace that was hardly relieved by plunging into a deep warm bath for two hours as soon as I got home.

It was there that I had time to plot and plan my next move.

The thought of joining the government department that had a nationwide deer culling operation under way certainly appealed as a possibility.

I was 16, and although I had never hunted deer, the thought of spending months in the mountains in isolated huts had quite an appeal to it. New Zealand has no predators, such as wolves or mountain lions, or even snakes, but deer had been imported from many countries over the past hundred years or so. They naturally proliferated to where they were designated a "noxious animal" - noxious, because they would come down from the high country to eat the precious grass that was so essential for the cattle and sheep industries.

Upping my game to use a .303, such as those we had used at Feilding Ag, wouldn't be a problem. They were the favored rifle among those government hunters, and most private hunters as well.

I was by now an excellent shot with a .22.

That came about because I learned a hard lesson when I shot my first rabbit. I had "borrowed" my father's single-shot .22 with the open sights so I could hunt along the banks of the Oroua river. Already something of an expert at target practice, I could hit the bull every time from the standing or prone positions.

However, rabbits don't always stay still. Some do. Some don't. This one must have seen me coming. It came out from under a Scotch Broom at a dead run. I panned, followed, and fired.

The bullet hit the poor creature in front of its hips. Its squeal of pain shocked me to the core. I picked it up by the back legs and finished it off with a "rabbit chop" to its neck. As I did so, I vowed I would become a much better shooter. In future I would always make a one-shot kill, but if that ever failed, I would never leave a wounded animal to suffer. I have kept that vow ever since.

I put aside the idea of becoming a government shooter, although in the years ahead I became an avid deer hunter, not for trophies, but for table meat. Although those days bare long gone, I can still drool over the taste of a Fallow deer back steak sliced and briefly cooked in garlic and butter, or a venison stew in red wine.

Sometimes I would pack out a 100-pound carcass to be sold to a buyer, who would then have it butchered in a pristine facility and send the venison to Germany.

In that warm bath, as the itching gradually went away, option two came to mind. What if I were to get a bit more serious about becoming a career newsman? If I did, I would become a real-life Randy Stone, gathering "the facts, ma'am, just the facts" as he would always say on his Saturday morning radio series. If I did, perhaps one day I would even have my own radio show.

Chapter 41

Captain Of My Ship

A s I LAY THERE, my father's "captain of my ship" quote came to mind.

I'm sure we've all had those difficult moments when something we've said gets misunderstood.

If it's a juicy piece of gossip, you can guarantee by the time it has circled the coffee table and then the neighborhood, the original can be totally unrecognizable.

This is well illustrated by imagining a British officer on the front lines of some war the "Empire" was engaged in. Lacking modern technology, he tells his underling officer to pass the order down the line verbally. "Send up reinforcements. We're going to advance."

By the time it gets to the end of the line, it has become "send up three and four-pence, we're going to a dance." (Silly, but you get the point).

My father liked to say he was quoting from Shakespeare when he said he was the captain of his ship. Not so. It was his version of the closing lines of the poem "Invictus" by William Ernest Henley. (Invictus is Latin for Unconquered).

The correct quote would be, "I am the master of my fate. I am the captain of my soul."

That poem has been an inspiration to many, including South Africa's Nelson Mandela, whose life was about abolishing apartheid, for which endeavor he spent many years in prison, but without losing hope or courage.

One can imagine Mandela in his solitary cell, buoyed by these lines during those many dark nights of the soul.

Chapter 42

INVICTUS

BY *WILLIAM ERNEST HENLY*

Out of the night that covers me,

Black as the pit from pole to pole,

I thank whatever gods may be,

For my unconquerable soul.

In the fell clutch of circumstance,

I have not winced nor cried aloud.

Under the bludgeonings of chance,

My head is bloody but unbowed.

Beyond this place of wrath and tears,

Looms but the Horror of the shade,

And yet the menace of the years

Finds and shall find me unafraid.

It matters not how strait the gate,

How charged with punishments the scroll,

I am the master of my fate,

I am the captain of my soul.

At 16, I knew nothing about the soul or the spirit. While I had read Shakespeare, my preference had shifted toward cowboy comics and stories by the likes of the late Zane Grey.

Call it escapism, which it was, but I often imagined being a cowboy in a white hat, In those fantasies I would be in the saddle, a Colt.45 slug in my shoulder, bleeding profusely as I rode away from a gunfight. The bad guy was back there on the ground. I was up on my horse, riding 50 miles to embrace the woman of my dreams.

There's nothing like dreaming of yourself as a hero while wallowing in a bathtub.

What I did know was that if I were to be the captain of my ship, I had to find a job on a newspaper.

I had heard of a newspaper called The Christchurch Star. It was head-quartered in the South Island city, Christchurch, where Byron was now spending a month or so as part of his aircraft engineering training for the National Airways Corporation.

I decided to go there, go to the Christchurch Star, and get a job.

However, before I get to that, I'm going to pretend that the following incident also came to mind as I lay in the tub. It was a close call and an education for both of us.

Chapter 43

Wellington Poofta

T HIS MEMORY IS ABOUT a time Byron and I took the train to Wellington. There, we learned a valuable lesson about the predilections of some men, which is probably why children are now taught the "Stranger - Danger" refrain.

Whatever the reason why we were there, we were just a couple of teenage country boys, totally innocent or perhaps simply ignorant about the world at large.

We disembarked from the train and took a seat on one of the wooden benches in the terminal.

A few minutes later, a rather well-dressed man rose from a seat across the way, came over and in a friendly manner inquired where we were from.

"Feilding."

"Oh. Have you been to the city and had a look around before?"

Naturally, the answer was "No. We haven't."

"Would you like to take a look?" he asked.

I looked at Byron. He looked at me. We silently decided, "Okay, let's have an adventure," and we told the man, "Yes."

Soon we were in a taxi, Byron in the middle as the three of us sat in the back seat. I gawked at the many shops and tall buildings in the downtown area, at the same time storing images of those on the corners whenever we turned up another street.

The man leaned forward and gave the driver some new instructions.

Turning to us, he said in a friendly voice, "You've come a long way. Would you like a sandwich at my place? It's just up here."

Our stomachs answered with a definite yes, although mine was hoping it wouldn't be a soggy lettuce and tomato one, or, worse still, peanut butter. I'd had enough of those when living at Hughie's place.

It surprised me a little when we were dropped off only a couple of miles from the railway station, yet on the outskirts of the capital. A capital it might be, but it was not a very big city at all.

The man then said, "Come in. I have to go to my room for a minute." He paused, then said, "Perhaps you should come with me. This is a boarding house and the landlady might wonder who you are if I leave you in the kitchen."

We followed him down a rather dark hallway to his small room, in which he had a single bed against the outside wall. A casement window just above it was slightly open, allowing a gentle breeze to waft the curtains back and forth.

He preceded us, invited us in, sat on his bed and opened a drawer in a small side table. From it, he retrieved a small bottle containing what looked like cold tea of the sort I had often taken to quench my thirst when hoeing mangolds.

Next came three of the smallest glasses I had ever seen.

Moving to the center of the bed, he motioned to Byron.

"Here, sit beside me here," he motioned to his left.

Byron did so.

I remained standing.

The man poured three glasses of tea, handed one to Byron, the next to me, and then, placing the bottle on top of the side table, he gave out a long sigh and said, "My word, I am quite tired you know. Perhaps I should lie down for a few minutes."

Byron had to stand, then sit again beside the man's head, at which the man took a half-sitting position and said, "Well, bottoms up."

Somehow, those words rang a warning bell in my mind as I put the tea to my lips.

My nose and lips and tongue rebelled at the smell and sting and taste of my first encounter with Scotch whiskey. I imbibed nothing but the merest sip.

Byron scoffed half his glass and almost immediately started acting like a very happy camper.

I was not.

My awareness was in overdrive.

I just knew without a doubt that we had to get out of there.

Seeing the man look at Byron with a funny expression, I moved to the foot of the bed, sat down facing Byron, and put the small glass in my left hand. While looking at Byron with the sternest look I could muster, I stretched my left hand and the glass to the far side of the bed. There, I tipped it enough to empty the contents while saying in a very definite tone of voice, "Byron, we have to get OUT of here."

Byron looked at me as if I was his dumb younger brother. Who was I to think he didn't know what was going on?

Putting me in my place with his big brother voice, he finished his whiskey in one short gulp, slapped his glass down on the side table and said "Let's RUN!"

Run we did. We thundered down the dark hallway and out into the bright sunlight.

We kept running, and whether or not he admitted it, Byron was surprised that I knew exactly what turns to take to get us back to the train station.

Chapter 44

Motorbikes

Having already digressed in the previous chapter about escaping a pedophile, although it would not be the last time, I might as well do it again, but on a very different subject.

Both horses and motorbikes have played a big part in my life. Bikes, in particular, have been significant because my dedication to motocross eventually taught me much about the power of the subconscious mind.

There was also a final major crash in which I died - and came back - but I'll save that story for another time.

I guess it was around 1958 while in our teens that Byron had a loan of a Francis Barnett two-stroke.

We had a lot of fun racing it around the house, except Byron wasn't happy with the sound of the engine. In a trice, he had a screwdriver in hand, adjusted a jet on the carburetor, and the bike sounded so much better.

Me, I was only interested in the riding part. We had both seen those daredevils riding the Wall of Death when the circus came to town.

Those high circular wooden towers would be erected overnight, and once we'd paid our entry fee, we could stand on a walkway at the top. Looking down, we would watch a man put on his helmet, jump on the bike, kick start it and sit there revving the engine.

With nowhere to go but up, the exhaust fumes reached the top of the wall of death. Two girls gagged and left. I almost gagged, but I stayed. I had paid good money to hopefully see this daredevil fall off the wall.

Engaging first gear, he began riding faster and faster around and around. Having changed gears and built up speed, at what he judged to be the right moment, he leaned sideways. Guiding the bike over a 45 degree circular ramp, he was onto the wall of death itself.

It was amazing to me that he didn't just fall off the wall. Relying on a fixed speed and centrifugal force, he could even ride up the wall to within a few feet of us spellbound boys, one of whom was so enthralled he just knew without a doubt that motorbikes were definitely on his wish list.

The Francis Barnett fulfilled that wish, even if only for a few days. Byron showed me how to use the clutch lever, the foot-operated gear lever, and the throttle that just needed a twist of the wrist to make the bike scream that it was ready to go.

This appealed to me immensely. Up till then, it had been a matter of delivering papers on a push-bike. As a budding stuntman myself, I could eventually stand on my bike on its back wheel and do a wheelie for a few yards.

This was a vast improvement over the day I had done my first solo bike ride at the age of seven or eight. Using a lady's bike because it had no crossbar,

I was finally able to stand on the pedals and pump them hard enough to gain enough forward momentum and balance to travel the length of the driveway.

Clearly, this called for an audience. I ran inside and said to anyone who would listen, "Come see! Come watch! I can ride a bike!"

Come watch, they did. They watched me proudly stand and pedal at least 15 feet. I was so proud of myself. I was grinning all over my face as I looked at them for approval, lost concentration focus and balance, and crashed into the hedge. I can hear their laughter now.

On the Francis Barnett, I started with a few wheel-spins and takeoffs on the lawn, then raced around the house to do it again.

Angry mothers can talk louder than a high-revving motorbike; "STOP THAT. GO SOMEWHERE ELSE" is a command one cannot refuse. "RIDE ON THE ROADSIDE IF YOU MUST," seemed like a very nice compromise.

It was then I decided it would be much more fun anyway to do a wheelie in the gravel beside the road. Byron would be hugely impressed. Once I was in position, front wheel on the tarmac, rear wheel in the gravel, I pulled in the clutch, kicked it into first, revved up, sat back, pulled on the handlebars, and let go of the clutch.

Byron told me later the wheelspin was awesome, although not as impressive as the next bit. The back wheel hit the tarmac, the front end leaped into the air, and I was thrown backwards to hit the road headfirst, cracking the side of my skull.

Although it hurt a lot and bled a lot, it wasn't broken.

Lesson learned the hard way (as usual) on every ride since that day I have worn a helmet and any piece of new body armor that came along. But even that didn't save me from knocking myself out in many future motocross and enduro races.

However, it was that decision to always wear at least a helmet that saved Byron's life. And mine too - more than once.

Chapter 45

"Where's My Bike!"

A YEAR OR SO later, Byron was pursuing his aircraft apprenticeship in Wellington, while I had worked hoeing mangolds and saved enough to buy a BSA C10 side-valve (whatever that meant).

One Saturday I decided to visit Byron, 100 miles away in the capital city.

A new white crash helmet, a pair of rubber gumboots and an oilskin parka were the only body armor I wore that day. The only reason I mention the boots is that while they looked the part, they had their shortcomings.

Cruising along at a boring top speed of about 50 miles an hour, I spotted a cardboard box on the berm up ahead. To relieve the boredom with a bit of fun, I guided the bike towards it, passed it on the right, and kicked it with my left foot.

Believe me, when my foot hit the road instead of the box, it was a lot more painful than kicking a hedgehog while wearing Roman sandals. My left leg flew backwards, and I almost lost control, just managing to veer back onto the highway while telling myself I would never do that again.

Byron was boarding some four miles from his work at the airport and was quite happy to pedal his push-bike there and back every day.

It was a pleasant enough ride around the coastline from Miramar where the tide would rise and fall over jagged rocks below the road. Seals could sometimes be seen basking in the sun, or penguins would waddle ashore after a trip from the Antarctic 2000 miles south.

I arrived to find him and his lifelong (thereafter) friend, Dave Hendricksen, singing and playing their guitars. What I was unaware of was that Byron had found himself a girlfriend, and the sight of my motorbike put a scheme in his head.

After admiring its blue paint and the sound of the engine, he asked, "Hey, can I borrow your bike? I want to go visit my girlfriend. She's a nurse at the hospital."

"Sure," I replied. "But make sure you wear the helmet."

"Thanks. See ya later," and off he went.

Like a mother worried about why her son hasn't come home, and it's midnight already (that was me and that's another story) I couldn't sleep as the hours ticked by.

I had some sneaky thoughts about what he might be up to with his girlfriend, but I was more concerned about my bike - and so I should have been.

About 2 in the morning, there was a thump on the door. I switched on the outside light, unlocked and opened the door, and there he was. In his left hand he had a grip on a crash helmet that had obviously saved his life. His face was all smashed up, there was blood all over his shirt, and aside from the ruby red liquid running from his nose, he was as white as a sheet.

I blurted out, "Where's my motorbike?"

Byron has a way of snorting when I say something unexpected. He snorted, which started his nosebleed afresh.

"On the rocks," he muttered through broken front teeth. "I fell asleep."

The rocks he was talking about were about 20 feet below the road. There were no corner barriers on that road, either. For my helmet to have been that smashed up, he must have hit the rocks headfirst, which meant he had likely been unconscious for quite a long time. Then he had to stagger on foot several miles back to the house.

It was an uphill battle for him to recover. He had knocked so much of his back out of place that he was bedridden for six weeks. Finally, our parents went and picked him up, brought him back to Feilding lying prone in the back seat of the old 1938 four-door Chevy (or was it the black Vauxhall?) and had him taken care of by a chiropractor.

The chiropractor worked miracles, as chiropractors have done for me over many decades and after many crashes of my own.

As for the motorbike, despite Byron's best efforts at putting it back together, it finished its life as a heap of junk.

When I eventually took up off-road racing, I almost finished up as a piece of junk myself.

Chapter 46

Knock Yourself Out

A DAY AT THE motocross races on a farm near Martinborough was one of the many events that prompted me to move to America.

Starting at age 37, I would buy a new dual purpose motorbike every year. By dual purpose, I mean they were designed for off-road racing, as well as city and highway riding. That meant they had a headlight, taillight, turn signals and a number plate.

I usually trailed the pack during weekend motocross events, eating their dust throughout the race. Consequently, I was often the last across the finish line. This was okay while I was getting the hang of it all. I would excuse my mediocre performance by convincing myself that "winners need followers, don't they, or they wouldn't be winners, would they?" You can only think like that until your brain plays switcheroo with your mind and suddenly there's a change in thinking. "Winners need losers, don't they?

"Who?

"Me?

"A loser?

"Hell NO!"

It was time to figure out how to be a winner.

Watching other starts I observed that those who got to the first corner first when the flag dropped or the light went green, often won the race, or were within the top five.

Getting to that corner ahead of 15 or 20 other riders was known as taking the hole shot.

I brooded on that for quite a while, reading motocross magazines between weekends, riding practice runs by myself, or testing myself with my trail-riding friends, the Belmont Trail Riders out of Lower Hutt.

I improved gradually, at least up to being one of the first 10 around the first corner. However, my ambition was to be the first there, and then the first across the finish line.

The breakthrough came when I read an article about a world-class racer who used a self-hypnosis system. He created an audio tape which he would listen to while drifting off to sleep, imagining how he would do this and that to win, or at least be among the first three at the end of his next event.

After buying a taped cassette version, I went to sleep every night listening to a soft-spoken voice with the sound of revving bikes as an underscore. The focus was on the very thing I wanted to achieve - victory at that first corner.

And achieve it, I did.

It happened at a Saturday event open to all-comers. This naturally meant the best riders in the district would be there.

The Yamaha 250 I had was relatively new. I had personalized it by moving the handlebars, so they were "just right" for the length of my arms, both sitting and standing. I changed the front fork oil to aid the suspension compared to my weight in the jumps and landings on the circuit.

Plus, it had a wrap-around bar that was bolted into the ends of the handlebars. Its purpose was to protect the turn signals and the clutch and brake levers in the inevitable "get off." A get-off meant a crash. I was very good at that too. And I was eventually good enough to be invited to the national motocross championship finals - not as a contender for the Big Trophy, but as a rider in the support races. I crashed in that as well.

However, getting back to that Martinborough event. I had spent a couple of weeks self-hypnotizing and visualizing my spectacular run to the first corner. There I would see myself using the side of the rut that previous races had built to lean my bike hard over, turn, then accelerate and leave the 19 guys behind me in a cloud of flying dirt and dust.

I also added a twist of my own to the start. I watched a couple of preceding races and carefully observed the body language of the guy with the starting flag. I noticed his right shoulder would twitch a second before he dropped the green flag, at which 20 screaming bikes would take off, heading as one for that coveted first corner.

Once lined up, with 19 bikes and riders in various shades of colored plastic armor, racing helmets and the latest in eye protection off to my left, I was exactly where I wanted to be. My plan was perfection itself.

I had an unobstructed view of the starter and his raised flag. I could clearly see his right shoulder. And from my right-side position, as soon as I was on the gas, I could drift left and force all the other riders to back off just enough to let me get to that first corner first.

Brilliant plan. Brilliant.

I kept an eagle eye on the starter guy.

His shoulder twitched.

Instantly, I simultaneously released the clutch and twisted the throttle to full, all in a split second.

Before that flag was down to his waist, I was two bike lengths ahead of everyone else.

Golfers would call it a hole-in-one. I won that hole shot.

I left them in the dust.

For about 25 yards.

Right there was the next obstacle - a 3 ft deep 4 ft wide trench with no dirt mounds on either side to provide a take-off rise to jump it. There was nothing in those hypnosis tapes about that.

As always, I had walked the track before the race, but I had been so focused on getting the hole shot that I had given no thought to what would come next and how I would handle it.

The correct procedure would be to sit back as far as possible, pulling the handlebars and the front end up off the ground, knowing that your speed would get you across the ditch. No problem. The back wheel and forks would handle the impact, the front wheel would hit the ground again, and you'd be off like a rocket.

At the rate I was traveling, I left all that far too late.

By the time I had moved my butt to the rear, the front end was over the ditch. I was about to do an endo (end-over-end).

Gravity pulled the front wheel straight down. It slammed into the far side of the ditch, which got the back end, and me, flying skyward. I just knew it was going to be a very hard landing.

Thankfully, I was wearing a very good crash helmet and the best plastic body armor one could buy.

My head hit the ground, and then my body did a forward roll all by itself. Flat on my back with all the wind knocked out of me, I recall looking up at blue sky while out of the corner of my eye I could see the front wheel of an oncoming bike.

The 19 bikes behind me were still close together, traveling at full throttle. The sound was deafening. Then it was bye-bye time. I blacked out.

I regained consciousness in a very quiet world. There was not a sound to be heard. Looking through my dusty goggles, I saw the face of someone looking down at me, asking for my name. It was the First Aid attendant.

I mumbled my name, then slowly stood up, noticing that I was surrounded by riders quietly waiting to hear whether I was alive or dead. I brushed myself off.

I was very much alive, and very grateful for that fact, considering that I had to brush off the tracks that had imprinted themselves on my chest, stomach and legs, evidence that at least three bikes had run over my unconscious body.

Didn't hurt a bit.

In fact, the blessing of it all was that I realized there was something powerful about those visualization techniques.

If I could visualize a hole shot, and get it, what else could I do with my mind?

Chapter 47

The Plane Truth

WITH HIS INNATE MECHANICAL aptitude, it was inevitable that Byron would find a trade requiring such skills.

I am sure he was also influenced by the fact that Dad had been an armorer in the Royal New Zealand Air Force (RNZAF). Byron began his apprenticeship at the local Tainui airport. It was not an airport in the modern sense. It lacked everything.

There was no sealed runaway, no control tower, no radar, no terminal building, no rip-off stores inside like you see at major airports around the world. Nor were there body scanners which today allow perverts to check your underwear and skeletal proportions.

No-one had yet heard of surveillance cameras and the facial identification crap that the modern world seems to accept without question. (Did you know that beards defeat those facial recognition cameras?)

The Tainui runway was nothing but a grassy field and an orange windsock to give incoming pilots a visual as to which way to land into the wind. The hangar was only a big old rusty barn with sliding doors wide and high enough to allow a topdressing plane to be pulled in out of the weather.

Topdressing, also known as crop-dusting, is the use of a specially designed plane to spread fertilizer on to grass pastures. This creates better and healthier growth.

Incidentally, at the time the Wright brothers were building their first flying machine in America, a young New Zealand farmer/inventor was also working on the same concept.

Wikipedia tells us "Richard William Pearse (3 December 1877–29 July 1953) was a New Zealand farmer and inventor who performed pioneering aviation experiments. Witnesses interviewed many years afterward describe observing Pearse flying and landing a powered heavier-than-air machine on 31 March 1903, nine months before the Wright brothers flew."

The Wright brothers flying machine first flew at Kitty Hawk, North Carolina, on December 17, 1903, with Orville at the controls.

Byron began his apprenticeship about 60 years later. During that time there had been many advances in airplane design, one of the most popular being to bi-wing Tiger Moth. They were popular with daredevils at country airshows, such as the one we attended at the Tainui airport.

We watched a daredevil fall out of the rear cockpit as the pilot did a barrel roll high above the field. Suddenly a parachute opened, and the daredevil could be seen pulling the parachute cords to adjust his descent. Once he hit the ground, he did a forward roll and sprang to his feet as the 'chute collapsed behind him. He quickly rolled it up and set it aside as the Tiger Moth came in for a landing.

Once again, the daredevil scooted into the rear cockpit. They took off once more, and on the next pass, just a few hundred feet above the gawking crowd, there he was, out on one of the Tiger Moth's wings, standing and waving to the crowd below.

With such an example, especially the landing under the parachute, I realized that a "parachute roll" must be added to my penchant for jumping off rooftops and out of trees. It worked extremely well. My knees never came up and hit me in the face ever again.

Now, where was I? Oh yes! Byron worked for a while at Tainui airport, then went on to further his apprenticeship in Wellington with the National Airways Corporation (NAC). As part of his education, he was also required to spend some months in Christchurch as well.

Perhaps I am now conflating events, but it's true to say that he was in Christchurch at the time I was dismissed from the Manawatu Times. And there I was, lying in the bathtub trying to recover from that terrible itching caused by those tiny shards of barley dust, pondering my future, and figuring out my next move to fulfill my ambition to become a reporter.

Why not go to Christchurch and get a job on a newspaper down there?

GREAT idea!

And if I took my precious Antoria guitar, Byron could teach me a few more chords, and maybe even how to sing proper.

Chapter 48

Star Struck - Out

RIDING THE TRANSIT BUS from the ferry terminal at Lyttelton into Christchurch, I had time to imagine how I would soon be more than a lowly copyholder.

A copyholder is not even the first rung of the ladder up the scale of journalism. A copyholder just holds the original copy that a reporter has written, while the proofreader drones on reading from the proof that has been typed out by the linotypers. Only when there is a discrepancy between the two can the copyholder speak, and the proofreader will make the necessary corrections.

My plan was that I would now become a cadet reporter on The Christchurch Star, work my way up to having my own beat, and eventually cover exciting assignments such as fires and accidents and city council meetings and court cases and write front-page stories.

But first I had to find a phone booth and call Byron at the number he'd sent me in his last and most infrequent of letters. That turned out well enough. I called from the bus station and found I was within walking distance from Byron's place, where he was boarding during his time in Christchurch.

Although the lady who owned the boardinghouse didn't seem too thrilled at my unexpected arrival, she had a spare bed and I was welcome to it, but the first thing she wanted to know was whether I had any money to pay for the privilege of living there. I did, which set her at ease, while I was more than happy to be back on dry land and able to sleep in a bed that didn't wallow and heave like my stomach had on the overnight ferry.

The next day I dressed in my best - a pair of jeans, my rather down-at-heel old black school shoes that I quickly polished as best I could with one of my socks, then donned a gray school shirt that had seen better days as well.

Borrowing one of the bikes the landlady had on hand, I headed for the unknown city center to find the office of the Christchurch Star. Not having thought to arrange an appointment in advance, it took a bit of talking to convince the receptionist that I was there to see the editor. In fact, she insisted he had a full schedule that day and I should perhaps come back some other time.

"That's okay," I said. "I'll wait." Saying which I sat down in a nearby chair and rolled a smoke. As I had learned at the Manawatu Times, being a smoker was synonymous with being a serious reporter, and I was more than willing to play the part.

My persistence paid off.

Only an hour later, the receptionist told me: "It must be your lucky day. He'll see you now - but only for 10 minutes." That was all I needed. Ten minutes from now, I would be in like Flynn.

It really was a very amicable 10 minutes. He listened politely as I told him about my extensive six months as a copyholder up north and how I had messed up and got fired, but now wanted a second chance and was ready to start work this very minute.

I like to recall his response this way.

He told me how much he appreciated my honesty. "But," he said, "I am fully staffed at the moment, so I'm afraid I don't have any immediate openings. However, I will start a file on you right now, and I'll get in touch as soon as something comes up."

With that, he took down my contact details, both locally, and those I gave him about my home address in the North Island. Then he placed those details in a manila folder, wrote my name, Bill Knight, on its identifying tag, opened the nearby filing cabinet, inserted it in its right place, closed the drawer, and turned to me with a genuine smile on his face.

"Thank you for coming in, young man. Or should I say, Bill? If anything comes up, we'll be in touch."

He shook my hand, walked me to the door, opened it, and showed me out.

His parting words were simply, "Good luck, son," and with that, my future had once again turned into a gray mist.

Once outside, I rolled another cigarette while my brain grappled with the fact that here I was in the Big City, with no job, just a couple of quid in my pocket but far from enough to get a return ticket on the ferry back north.

What was I to do?

I jumped on the bike and started riding around the city, naturally upset that my dream hadn't come true, but doing my best to put things into perspective so I could figure out what to do next.

Chapter 49

Irish Wisdom

As I pedaled past the Christchurch Cathedral, which had been a tourist attraction for many decades, I recalled a family legend. It was said that my paternal grandfather had passed through here before the First World War.

My memory of the story is probably not entirely accurate, but it's worth telling and it goes something like this.

Granddad Knight was born in Ireland. The name Knight was said to have been a contraction and English pronunciation of the Spanish Iknight. Supposedly, his paternal Spanish ancestor had been lucky enough to survive and swim ashore in Ireland when the Spanish armada, on its way to destroy England, was literally blown apart by a huge storm.

Like much of the history we are taught these days, careful research will reveal that a lot of what we believe about the past is quite incorrect. Sometimes it is even fake. There is certainly a great deal more to history than we have been allowed to be aware of.

I have researched the word "Iknight," in order to verify that part of the family legend, but the name cannot be found on the Internet. Instead, you find that "knight" translates to or from the Spanish "caballero." However, the general description remains the same. Caballeros and knights were warriors, and that is certainly what my grandfather was.

They say he was disillusioned with Catholicism in Ireland and ran away to England when he was 14. There, he enlisted in the British army by lying about his age. At some point, so the story goes, he took up boxing and eventually became British Empire middleweight boxing champion. I am sure he passed on those fighting genes to my father, and to me.

He also abhorred injustice. During his spell in the British army, he became appalled at the vicious punishments meted out by the officers of the time, so he deserted. He did so knowing full well that if caught, the punishment would be death by firing squad.

Somehow, he was able to join the crew of a tramp steamer, working as a stoker all the way to Cape Town in South Africa. There, he jumped ship, intending to disappear inland, but he was apprehended and returned to the ship, which then sailed for New Zealand and the port of Lyttelton.

Having learned his lesson in South Africa, this time he put a couple of loaves of bread in a sack and started walking, stopping only briefly at times, until he was at least 100 miles from port.

But then, the First World War started, and the king was calling for more troops to man the trenches, promising deserters that if they should return and serve in the army, they would not be shot.

Is that an irony or what? Return and get shot at and you will not be shot for deserting! Was that Irish logic or what? And did I inherit those genes as well?

After returning to England, Granddad spent several years in the artillery in France and elsewhere. He did not get shot. But he did get mustard gassed. This near-death experience had him repatriated to England for intensive care. Fighting for his life, he is said to have asked why red curtains would suddenly appear around some beds of other mustard-gassed patients.

The answer was that there was nothing further that could be done for them, so they were curtained off and left to their inevitable fate while attention was turned to doing everything possible for those not so far gone.

It was an honest and timely answer, for it enabled my grandfather to understand his personal situation the morning he woke to find his bed surrounded by red curtains.

I think willpower, coupled with prayer, is what pulled him through.

He survived, married his nurse, and emigrated back to New Zealand.

They settled in Palmerston North, where he became a lay preacher, first in the Exclusive Brethren (which he quit when they raised a fuss over a woman wearing lipstick to a Sunday service) and then within the Open Brethren.

As for myself, although I had had a religious upbringing, by the time I was riding past the Christchurch Cathedral, I was an agnostic, which would before long turn to atheism.

I was also on my own, out of work, and almost broke. I needed to get grounded and find a job.

Wondering what to do, I stopped riding, sat on a nearby bench, pulled out my tobacco and papers, and started rolling a smoke.

As I was about to lick the ZigZag paper to complete the job, I paused and stopped. I carefully returned the pinch of tobacco to its pouch, discarded the now useless paper, and stuffed the pouch and matches back in my pocket.

Until I could find work, and even if I found a job this very day, it would be at least a week before any new money would come my way. I definitely had to conserve my tobacco.

Chapter 50

Monkey Business

R ATHER THAN BACKTRACK THE way I had come into the city, I chose to try a couple of side streets.

Taking a different route on the spur of the moment has been a lifelong habit because I have found that following the same path all the time gets as boring as anything you can imagine. Like riding the bus to school, day in and day out, nothing new seems to happen when you follow the same routine day after day after day.

Such simple decisions as turning left or right can really lead to big life-changing encounters and events. This I would certainly experience once I moved to America, but we'll get to that, eventually.

While I have long forgotten the name of the car dealer business that I was about to pass on the Christchurch street I had chosen to take, I have never forgotten the sign outside it on which, in rough handwriting, were the words "Grease Monkey Wanted."

Ten minutes later, I had a job.

I was the company's new grease monkey.

Now perhaps I should spell out what a grease monkey is, or at least, was. Cars of that era required grease in numerous locations to prevent undue wear and tear on various metal components. Where required, a small grease nipple was available to take either a needle-nosed or overlapping fitting attached to a hand-held gun that contained the grease.

Homeowners who preferred to do their own mechanical work would have dug a pit in their garage so they could get underneath their vehicles. My father had dug one of those in the garage he'd built at our Palmerston North home. He racked up a lot of miles on his mail runs and needed to keep his cars, or eventually a Bradford van, in good shape.

However, this garage in Christchurch was far more modern. It had a drive-on hoist that would lift the vehicle to a height of six feet, leaving room underneath for the "grease monkey" to check every nook and cranny for those grease nipples, or drain and change the engine oil.

It was the sort of work you could train a monkey to do. Perhaps they should have hired one.

The reason I recall the hoist would raise a vehicle only six feet is that I discovered on my first day on the job that this was a real drawback. Having grown six inches in six months when I was 14, I was now over 6 ft tall. I spent that first day ducking under cars, awkwardly groping around driveshafts and axles and wheels to find those points that needed grease, and banging my head everywhere. By the time I got home, my hair was full of grease and dirt. So I bought a cap, which worked very well, except that the cap, and my height, eventually had me fire myself.

That's right. I fired myself.

Not only was that company set up to service all makes and models of cars, it was also an agent for and importer of two models of new Renault vehicles from France. The bigger of the two had something like 30 grease nipples underneath, if I recall correctly, whereas the smaller one took just a few minutes to service.

New Zealand law required all vehicles to have a Warrant of Fitness, renewable every six months, for a fee, at a local testing station. I had been on the job for a couple of weeks when the foreman had me take a customer's older Renault to get a warrant.

The car was in good shape and easily passed the inspection.

As I left, I turned left onto the street, then gunned it, intending to show my teenage driving prowess and burn rubber or do a smoky doughnut.

Suddenly, there was a sound like a rifle shot. The engine revved like crazy while the car inexplicably slowed down.

As quick-thinking as your average turtle, I slowly realized the car was going nowhere. With what forward motion remained, I steered it alongside the kerb. I parked it and walked back to the garage, wondering what to tell the foreman. I was definitely not going to say I had over-revved the engine, dropped the clutch, and expected to do a wheelspin down the road. So I simplified the truth. I said, "Sorry I'm late back. Had to walk. Seems an axle snapped on that old car" (emphasis on the "old"), and left it at that.

No doubt you can guess that a simplified truth can also be a half-truth, or as I would eventually discover, a simplified truth is sometimes only five percent of the story.

The foreman was good enough to take my word for it without further question, although I suspected from the way his eyes rolled and squinted that he knew there was more to the story than I was telling.

Indeed, there was, but on this occasion, the fix wasn't too difficult. They had the car towed back and fitted with a new axle well before the owner came to pick it up - no comment and no charge.

A couple of weeks later, I was tasked with taking another small Renault for a warrant. This was one of their brand new imports. It was shiny and good looking and the interior smelled of that soft new vinyl lining that was all the rage.

I drove carefully to the testing station, got the warrant, and drove sedately back to park the car in the showroom as instructed. I parked strategically near the showroom window because even though it was a pre-sold vehicle, letting the passing public see it might entice them in to become buyers themselves. Pleased with myself for thinking about the firm and job security, I switched off, opened the door, and began to step out.

It was then that my world stopped for a second or two, before my head started spinning - metaphorically - because it was sticking to the brand new top-class off-white soft vinyl hood lining.

The ugly reality was that I had neglected to remove my grease monkey cap before taking the car for testing. And now there was a huge smothering of grease soaking into the vinyl above my head.

This, I knew, was certainly grounds for divorce. I knew I was going to be fired when I confessed my oversight to the foreman. In fact, even though it was payday tomorrow, he might just kick me out the door and send me on my way with nothing but curses ringing in my ears instead of payment for my last week on the job.

What to do?

I walked over to the accountant's office, told him, "I don't know whether you've heard, but I'm finishing up. Can you make out my check? I'll be back in a few minutes."

He looked a little nonplussed but said, "Yeah, right. Okay," and reached for the pay register and a checkbook.

I walked back past that 6 ft hoist, told the foreman the whole truth and nothing but the truth, apologized, picked up my check, threw my dirty grease monkey cap into the trash, jumped on my bike and started pedaling furiously while thinking: "Well, that's that. What's next? I need work!"

Once again, I chose a different road, and it was thanks to that split second decision and the millions of sheep that make their way as carcasses and wool to far distant places that I had a new job within 30 minutes.

Chapter 51

Woolstore Interlude

IN MAPPING AND DESIGNATING locations and boundaries for cities and provinces, the settlers used a combination of Maori and English names. In the South Island there is the province of Canterbury, within which lies the city of Christchurch.

Canterbury, like much of the rest of New Zealand, supports many sheep farms.

As I would discover when I eventually owned a small farm myself, green grass and sheep are better than money in the bank. For one thing, you can eat sheep, but you can't eat money. Nor is money self-replicating, which is something sheep do every year, and grass does all the time.

Therefore, I realized that grass is green gold. It feeds sheep, which grow wool and meat and, because of those attributes, New Zealand developed a major trading arrangement with Britain.

Although they were at opposite ends of the earth, this proved to be a good thing, because the seasons are reversed. Winter in Britain is summer in New Zealand, where farmers realized they could time their breeding to produce the best lamb carcasses to send to Britain in time for the Christmas demand. Second: There was a global demand for wool. It had become a multi-million dollar (or pounds or yuan) industry.

It was this product that got me my next job.

The new road I chose after quitting my job as a grease monkey took me into the industrial zone. I found myself cycling past an enormous building where flatbed trucks were being loaded with bales of wool. On the spur of the moment, I parked the bike, walked inside, and asked if they had any work.

Next minute I was pushing what's called a "skip," a monster six-wheeled barrow, full of wool.

This was one of many such operations in New Zealand before the nylon and synthetic alternatives became widely available.

Wool was universally used for such things as warm clothing, socks, long-johns, shirts, scarves, felt hats, blankets, coats, sweaters, and the ubiquitous Swanni - a hooded pullover coat that for decades has been favored by farmers and outdoors-men throughout the country.

Buyers, including many from overseas, China among them, would attend annual auctions. They were looking for wool of particular grades of fineness. This was important according to its destined end use. For this reason, the fleeces had to be sorted into classes, depending on the size of the fibers and the breed of the sheep, and that is what a Wool Classer would spend his days doing.

My job was simply to stand by for the little time it took for the classer to evaluate a fleece, then throw it in my skip which, once full, I would trundle over to the wool press, where it would be baled, stamped with the appropriate identification, and sent off to the loading bays.

While I seriously thought about becoming a wool classer myself, it was clearly seasonal work, aside from which the thought of an eight-hour day standing in one spot held no appeal whatsoever.

I had no idea that I would soon become the youngest Chief Reporter in New Zealand newspaper history.

Chapter 52

First Up Best Dressed

BYRON LEFT HIS BICYCLE with me when he returned to Wellington to continue his apprenticeship, while I left that boarding house, having found a place closer to my work.

In the boarding house I moved to, I shared a rather large upstairs dormitory with three Maori guys about my age who also had work in the area. We became reasonably cordial companions, although it was through them I learned the meaning of the phrase, "first up, best dressed."

Using my earnings from the wool store, had bought a good leather jacket, a pair of leather motorcycle boots, and a new pair of jeans.

I got up one Saturday morning to find my jacket, boots, and jeans had disappeared, as had my three roommates.

Our room had a big casement window on the street-facing wall, and it was open. Through it, I heard their familiar laughter. I went to the window, and there they were, on the footpath, rolling their morning cigarettes and laughing and joking about the prank they had just pulled.

Below me, wearing my clothes, were Maaka (the Maori version of Mark), Rangi (sky, or god of the sky), and Ihaka (he will laugh).

Maaka was wearing my boots, Rangi, my jacket, and Ihaka my jeans that didn't quite fit. They almost doubled up with glee when I shouted down to them, "Oi! I need to get dressed and go to work!" I too laughed, but not entirely happily.

It was early November, which meant that up north the mangolds would soon need thinning, and I knew for certain I could get work there. I decided to leave Christchurch, which would mean biking to Lyttelton to catch the ferry, and that was a decision that carried a lesson. I had accumulated more stuff, including a backpack that served as my wardrobe and carryall. However, I couldn't wear that on my back and somehow carry my guitar as well while biking to Lyttelton.

Having told the boys I was heading out, Rangi said he too was planning to go north a few days after me, once the ferry had returned to Lyttelton. He offered to bring my guitar with him, get in touch if I gave him my home phone number, and he would catch the train from Wellington, which always stopped at Feilding, and he'd meet me there to give me my guitar.

This seemed ideal to my naïve young mind, so I agreed.

I never heard from him, nor saw my guitar, ever again.

My next guitar, a Yamaha, was waiting for me in America about 30 years in the future - and I still have it 30 years later.

Chapter 53

The Elvis Influence

ACK HOME FROM CHRISTCHURCH, I found my parents had finally separated.

That was a good thing as far as I was concerned, because their example of married bliss was exactly the opposite of what I intended to create in my future. I would meet and marry the woman of my dreams and I would be the perfect husband and father. But first, I had a few things to attend to, such as hoeing mangolds for another season.

It was good to be back in the open air, bare feet in the dirt and the sun tanning my body a healthy copper color from long hours of exposure to its ultraviolet rays.

I bought my first transistor radio and a belt and pouch so I could have it with me and listen to the news. I listened to Randy Stone on Saturday mornings, and the songs from the Top 100 that frequently featured Elvis Presley.

I was an Elvis fan in the process of developing my own teenage persona. Who could be a better role model than the good-looking man with a distinctive and seductive voice, gyrating hips, and sensuous lips?

Images of myself an Elvis lookalike washed through my brain.

Little did I know that the images associated with thought are the seeds of creation. The images are created in the mind the invisible etheric world - and what we think and imagine in the invisible creates our future. To put it bluntly, it can be said that, for better or worse, we brainwash ourselves.

I soon created my future in the physical world by buying a pair of light blue jeans, a classy pink shirt, and a pair of new wingtip shoes, tan-colored with thick soles. I personalized them with drawing pins inserted all around the sole. To my mind, they looked like silver conchos and were very classy indeed.

That was my go-to-town outfit for Friday nights. Because there were less than 20 shops in all of Feilding, there was a lot of slouching back and forth to ensure I was noticed in my fine regalia.

Fuddy-duddy adults would look down their noses as I passed by, some of them muttering to each other, "I just don't know what the world is coming to!"

Ignoring their disapproving eyes, a cigarette jutting from one side of my mouth, I would raise my upper lip on the other side slightly. It was a perfect copy of that sensual look that Elvis was so good at.

It worked for me. On one occasion, a car slowed down, and a good-looking teenage Maori girl leaned out the window, laughing as she and her girlfriends invited me to a party.

I wasn't expecting the party to be in another town, nor that I would spend the night alone on a threadbare couch in a broken-down house. Worse still, the next morning, no one could remember who I was or how I got there.

My "friends" who had picked me up were nowhere to be seen. It was a long walk to the local intercity bus station, and an endless talk from my irate mother when I finally got home.

Foreigners who came to visit New Zealand were known to say they needed to set their clocks back 50 years, so far behind the rest of the world were New Zealand and its people. Shops opened only from 9 to 5 Monday to Thursday, 9 till 8 on Fridays for "late night shopping" and closed at weekends. Saturdays were for rugby and cricket, or lawn bowls if you were old and retired. Sundays were for church and picnics.

Most husbands could support a family, including four kids, by working a 40-hour week. Wives were for having children (practicing frequently) and diligently looking after the home front. They would make sure that everyone went to whatever church they belonged to on Sundays, said grace at every meal, especially over the Sunday dinner of roast lamb, potatoes peas, and carrots. If the family's free-range chickens were productive enough, the whites of their eggs would make a pavlova dessert topped with real whipped cream and passion-fruit.

Our family wasn't quite like that. According to my mother, with Dad gone, he just wasn't sending enough alimony home to meet all the bills. Therefore, I was quite happy to give her a big percentage of my wages. After all, I was now "the man of the house" and since I had been such an advocate of my parents getting divorced, I felt it was now my responsibility to look after my mother and my three younger brothers and sister.

This worked well for several months until the day a mysterious letter arrived. It was addressed to Bill Knight, 231 Kimbolton Rd, Feilding, and was stamped and postmarked "Westport."

Having learned to draw a map of New Zealand freehand in geography classes, I knew Westport was on the West Coast of the South Island. The West Coast is notorious for its rainfall of 200 inches a year.

Despite that, it had been settled initially by men who had heard - when the California gold rush was petering out - that there was "gold in them thar hills" in New Zealand. In reality, it was mostly in the West Coast rivers and streams, which was relatively easy pickings back then, but that too eventually petered out.

That's all I knew about the West Coast. I certainly did not know anyone from that part of the country.

The letter was from the Editor of The Westport News, offering me the job of Chief Reporter. He said accommodation had been arranged at a local boarding house, and my responsibilities would be to report on local council meetings and seasonal sports, including rugby and cricket.

Requesting that I be there as soon as possible, he wrote that I could get a free ride from Nelson (top of the South Island) to Westport. There was a man who did a nightly run to dispense copies of the Nelson Evening Mail to the small settlements along the way.

Within 24 hours, I was on the move.

I packed my suitcase with a change of clothes, including a new pair of the latest fashion in stovepipe trousers. They had a sparkly, light greenish sheen to them. Next, my wingtip shoes wrapped in newspaper, and my pink shirt.

Last, a rose-pink silk bandanna that had looked really great in the mirror as I carefully tied it as a cravat around my neck. Elvis never looked so good. My travel clothes simply comprised blue jeans, a gray shirt and sweater, and those down-at-heel black school shoes.

This time I paid for my train ticket to Wellington, arrived in time to catch the Inter-Island ferry to Picton, and from there hitched a ride across the top of the South Island to Nelson.

The driver was good enough to drop me off at the offices of the Nelson Evening Mail, where I asked permission to hang out through the night until my ride was ready to go in the early hours.

About 3.30 or 4 in the morning, my somewhat reluctant chauffeur shook me awake and introduced himself rather tersely. I understood why once he had me sit in the passenger seat. Adding me and my suitcase to his usual load of newspapers was indeed an enormous challenge. My presence clearly upset his usual system of placing two bundles of newspapers onto the passenger seat. To deal with that inconvenience, he dumped them in my lap.

As we headed south, the smell of freshly printed newspapers reminded me of my few short months on the Manawatu Times, and an indelible memory of my father and a quirky smile.

Chapter 54

Lead Story

P LEASE DON'T FEEL YOU'VE been misled.

This is not about a lead story on a paper.

It is a story about the metal kind of lead.

Therein it qualifies as a lead story.

Wondering how my limited, almost non-existent experience so far would fit me for my duties as a chief reporter in Westport, I had a nagging suspicion that I would prove to be a misfit there as well.Should I have phoned the Editor and turned the job down? Perhaps.

But what if this was the golden opportunity I had been waiting for?

Would I crash and burn this time as well?

Yes, I had been a misfit on the Manawatu Times. My potty-mouth explosion had cost me that job. Vowing not to do that again and putting aside any self-recriminations, I commended myself for having learned how to type quickly with two fingers.

Every good reporter did that, so it surely meant I had made a start, and the editor of the Westport News would be impressed with that skill at least.

I had another skill that would also be useful. I knew how to make lead plates for a printing press. On the Manawatu Times, after practicing typing from 2 to 4 in the morning, I would then help the men who kept the press running.

My job was to pick up the heavy lead plates that had been cast and used the previous night, and slide them carefully into the big open-topped vat in which liquid lead was bubbling at over 500 degrees Fahrenheit. There they would melt into their liquid lead form, ready to be recast for that day's issue of the paper.

Each plate was a reverse copy of a page in the newspaper, shaped in a half-round to fit the rollers in the press. They weighed - well, they were a lead weight, and there was a knack to picking them up, resting them on the edge of the vat, and controlling their slide into the bubbling cauldron.

On one occasion, I goofed. A plate slipped from my grasp and splashed into the vat, sending molten lead droplets shooting in all directions, including onto my wrist. It immediately lodged in the steel band of my wristwatch, instantly giving me a third-degree burn.

My silence was enough to tell the observing foreman it hurt like hell. He quickly grabbed the nearby first aid box, somehow got my watch off my wrist, slathered something on the burn, then said "best leave it in the open air," before adding, "guess you'll be more careful now, right?" and put me back to work.

As soon as the press was fired up and running, filling the air with its deafening roar as it pounded out newspaper after newspaper, I would move to the area where mail runners like my father would perform the next act in this daily routine.

They would pick up a stack of papers, still warm from being printed and collated in whatever size or number of pages were required that day. Then they would roll them one by one into a pre-glued paper binder. This took about 30 seconds, each paper then being a miniature missile ready to slide into a subscriber's letterbox with the mail, or be thrown into the driveway on the way past if there was no mail for that address.

I usually had all Dad's papers rolled and ready by the time he arrived. Quickly throwing bundles onto the back seat, he would instruct me with the usual two words, "Get in," and drop more papers in my lap. Then it was off to the races.

Gravel roads made up much of his run and he honestly reveled in driving as fast as possible wherever he could, sliding sideways through a turn, correcting and sliding the other way as he rounded the next corner.

He also had a show-off streak. Alongside many mailboxes were shelves on which were empty glass milk bottles, washed and waiting to be exchanged for full ones to be delivered by some other contractor.

I recall it well. Cars in New Zealand are right-hand drive, which was fine for a right-handed former rugby player who needed to keep his window down so he could throw newspapers into driveways on both sides of the road as he sped by. He always timed the pitch so well that the paper landed exactly where intended - on the driveway and not in the roadside ditch.

On this day, the driveway involved was off to the left. That meant he must extend his arm out of his window and throw the paper across the bonnet (or hood, as it's called in America).

Perhaps because things weren't going so well at home, he was driving much faster than usual. Whatever the reason, be it a deliberate bit of anger release, or perhaps just showing off, what he did has been a slow-motion memory ever since.

Sliding full-speed and sideways around a sharp right-hand turn, he had his foot down on the gas, his left hand deftly spinning the steering wheel to the left to hold the slide exactly where he wanted it.

Knowing my place, I handed him a newspaper. Leaning slightly forward, he extended his right arm out the open window. Cocking his head slightly left and forward, he sighted in on his target. Like a boxer throwing a powerful right, he threw that paper across the front of the car.

It sped across the road and scored a bullseye hit.

Four milk bottles instantly turned into broken shards of flying glass.

As he straightened out of the slide, leaving behind a trail of dust, flying gravel and broken glass, his sideways look at me, his left cheek sort of puckered up in a half-grin, was all that needed to be not said.

The man who was taking me to Westport was far more sedate.

Chapter 55

The Westport News

BECAUSE OF MANY STOPS along the way, the drive from Nelson to Westport, which are only about 100 miles apart, seemed to take a very long time.

Having hardly slept at all since leaving Feilding many hours before, it was easy enough to doze off between stops to drop off papers here and there. We passed through Richmond, Hope, Belgrove, Motupiko, Glenhope, Longford, Murchison, Inangahua, and the Buller Gorge, and finally into Westport itself.

Westport is a small coastal town at the mouth of the Buller River, where it meets the Tasman Sea. First surveyed a hundred years previously (in 1862) Westport had seen a short-lived gold mining era, but was now better known for its coal mining and fishing industries. The coastal sand was also an important resource, an essential ingredient in concrete and cement.

We arrived around 7 in the morning. The driver stopped in the main street outside a weather-beaten old place on which the words "Westport News" had been written many years before.

Motioning me to step out, he walked around the car, opened the rear door, and said, "Here. Help me with these." "These" were several big bundles of newspapers, each headlined "Westport News."

The penny dropped. The paper was printed on the Nelson Mail press and transported to Westport. . was down to only one skill - two-finger typing.

Knowing the town well, the driver then dropped me off at the widow's home where I would be a boarder. She showed me to my room, offered a cup of tea and a bowl of porridge for breakfast, and then it was time to meet the Editor of the Westport News.

Quickly changing into my best clothes, I headed for the newspaper office.

I walked through the front door at precisely nine o'clock.

At one minute past, I was in the newsroom looking at a man dressed in a slightly crumpled charcoal suit, white shirt, and a plain semi-matching tie.

He looked up from his typewriter, tapped a few more keystrokes (with two fingers), rolled the copy paper out, and laid it alongside the typewriter.

Still wearing that quizzical look that had taken over his face as I came through the door, he said, "Who are you?"

"Bill Knight."

"Bill, WHO?" he said, his voice rising somewhat.

"Bill Knight. The new chief reporter."

Neither of us said anything for the next endless minute. Yet I am sure our separate thoughts were happening much faster than any words can express them.

Speaking for myself, I was feeling just a tad miffed. Here I was dressed in my best, my shiny stovepipes, pinkish shirt, cravat, and even my conch-studded wingtips I had carefully wiped with my hanky that very morning.

And here was this guy, this Editor, in a rumpled charcoal suit and white shirt and tight tie on a warm summer morning, looking at me as if I was something the cat dragged in.

Taking off his tortoiseshell glasses, laying them alongside the Olivetti, he stood up, removing his jacket as he did so. It was then I noticed the thinning elbows and the threadbare cuffs. His white shirt looked freshly ironed, which suggested he was married, whereas mine was rumpled from having been rolled in my suitcase, and for me the last thing on my mind was marriage. Love would be good. But marriage? Nah!

It was Friday morning.

"Okay," he said. "You've come a long way. Take the day off. Walk around town. Introduce yourself to people. Get to know the place a bit."

"Yes, SIR!" I responded, using the word "sir" for the first time since quitting school, where every teacher had to be addressed with at least the veneer of respect implied by that word. I never used it outside of school, nor would I salute my so-called superiors, which was why I had been told not to come back to cub scouts when I was 8, and kicked in the butt by my father for not saluting a so-called NCO when I was 13. Of such temperament are misfits made.

But this time, it seemed smart to say "Yes SIR!" because I sensed that to get off on the right foot, I needed to counter that strange look he'd given me, which was probably why he made that quick shift into being polite and giving me the day to get to know the town and some of its people.

Looking back, I can say that I fit into the social life in Westport much better than I fit into the newsroom, where, within a few days, I was genuinely feeling out of place.

I did not know how to write a short sentence to start a report. My two-finger typing was still slow, and the editor had trouble keeping his eyebrows in place as he shuffled through my work.

One paragraph per sheet of copy paper was the rule back then. This was a practical convenience for reporters, copy editors and subeditors who determined the flow and length of the story. It also meant that while I was typing up my stories, I could discard any paragraph where I might have misspelled just one word, which I often did, and start over. Naturally, this was time consuming, and I soon noticed it bothered the editor more than just a little.

He was polite, but distant, which meant he was most unlikely to become a bosom buddy if I were to work for this paper for any length of time. I decided all I needed was a few months to learn the basics, and then I could leave this Podunk little town and take my skills to a much more prestigious newsroom.

Meanwhile, common sense made sense. After that first meeting, which had the editor's eyes looking at each other so he could avoid looking at my obviously heathenish teenage attire, I made a point of only wearing my much more acceptable but rather dowdy clothes to work. It comprised those old black school shoes, a gray shirt and pullover, and a pair of matching longs with nice straight creases, thanks to the widow allowing me to use her ironing board.

After that first foray around town, Fridays and Sundays were my days off. Saturday was a workday because I was to be assigned to cover the local cricket match, the accurate results of which were of the utmost importance to the Editor, and to the paper's subscribers.

Naturally, the names of the teams and the players, their positions on the field, who batted and who was the bowler and who was bowled out with his wickets skittled or because he was caught LBW (leg before wicket) were all grist for the (accurate) mill. I'll come back to that.

On my first Friday off, I dressed in my spiffy clothes. As expected, they certainly got the attention of one or two (or maybe more) young women, one of them given to wearing her own version of trendy attire - a tight-fitting dress cut in Chinese style which suited her nickname, Suzie Wong.

By the time my second Friday off came around, we were on good speaking terms and she and her girlfriend invited me to a party.

Someone's parents were away, so the plan was to have a couple of guys buy several one-gallon flagons of beer and we could have a good time.

Indeed, it was, but only until the party came to a very sudden halt.

Two of the guests were on a break from their jobs as government hunters. Cullers they were known as, since their job was to live in the hills for a month or two at a time, shooting (culling) deer and taking their tails as evidence of how many they had shot.

Private hunters could also trade a deer's tail for three rounds of .303 ammunition. The .303 with its open iron sights had been the favored military rifle and was cheap enough that most government hunters used them. The government apparently had millions of bullets to give away in the belief that this would make a dent in the numbers of deer and Wapiti (the imported American elk) that bred so prolifically in the Southern Alps.

As we drank beer and yahoo'd around, dancing badly to whatever was on the radio, those two young men started arguing. One was saying some of his tails had disappeared. The other took umbrage at the accusation, and in a trice, fists were flying.

Placing myself between them and Suzie and her girlfriend, I spread my arms and shepherded them back into a corner. As I did so, I saw another girl race into the hallway and pick up the wall-mounted phone. "I'm calling the police," she said breathlessly.

It was the shorter of the two who got the upper hand. Perhaps he had some wrestling background, for he lunged at his opponent, grabbed him around the waist, lifted him off his feet and body slammed him between the floor and the wall.

The look of shock and horror on the downed man's face is with me to this day.

The body slam had been accompanied by the squishy sound of breaking glass and a fountain of beer that spurted out from under his back. He had been slammed onto a full flagon, and now his back was fast oozing beer and losing blood.

"Oh, shit!" said the short one. "We've got to get you to the hospital." Enmity was instantly forgotten as he helped the wounded guy to his feet. When last seen, they were stumbling out to someone's car, while the rest of us were walking away as quickly as we could, knowing the local one and only policeman could be there at any minute.

Three weeks into my job, I was assigned to cover an important cricket match. The editor provided me with the sacred book of record in which he had jotted down columns of notes and names and other jargon when covering previous matches.

By now, my friendship with Suzy was progressing very well, though not yet as far as I had fantasized. With that in mind, but keeping it to myself, I invited her to attend the match with me. She accepted, and with a tiny sense of self-importance, I led the way into the stand, where we took a couple of seats well away from the rest of the fans.

The game got under way at the same time that everything I thought I knew about cricket disappeared from my brain. Opening the book the editor had entrusted me with did no good at all. I was completely flummoxed.

Even worse, whoever the live commentator was, he was speaking a very foreign language. Nor did Suzie help with her own vocal commentary as she said things like "Oh look. The bowler is using backspin with a bit of side. See how the ball hits the ground and bounces up sideways?"

There was nothing I could say, but I took a note of what she had said because it would at least look good when I wrote the game up back at the office.

I came in to work on Monday morning to find the editor already at his desk, working on my report of the match while running his fingers down the columns I had filled in in the book of record. Once again, his eyebrows were going up and down and his eyes were looking at each other.

Motioning to a chair in front of his desk, he removed his glasses and said, "Take a seat."

I took a seat.

"Your name really is Bill Knight?" he asked.

"Of course it is," I replied. "For the last 17 years," I added, rather unnecessarily.

He let that slide.

"Did you ever apply for a job on the Christchurch Star?"

Well, that was a dumb question!

"Yes. And they're going to get in touch when they have a vacancy, so I'm afraid I may not be here too long."

He let that pass too, then said: "Well, I know the editor of the Star, and when I was looking for a reporter, I spoke to him myself."

"He's a good man," I chipped in.

Again, it was as if I hadn't said a word.

"And he said he'd send me a file so I could contact one of his ex reporters, a guy by the name of Bill Knight."

That was certainly a new one on me. I was not an ex-reporter from the Christchurch Star, so instead of responding, I pulled out a smoke and lit up, wondering where this was going.

"Now you've been here three weeks, right? And you've done your best."

He paused, lit a cigarette of his own, inhaled, then exhaled smoke in my direction.

"But you don't know anything about reporting, do you?"

That might have been the truth, but as they say, the truth, hurts, so I did a big drawback and coughed mightily as I exhaled.

He carried on.

"So I called the Star editor again, and it turns out there are two Bill Knights. And there were two files in his filing cabinet. And he sent me yours instead of the other one."

I was taking my cigarette packet out of my shirt pocket with my left hand and stubbing out my current cigarette with my right at this point.

"TWO of me!" I was thinking. "Well, that's GREAT because he (whoever he is) got me this job."

Using a word that I'd have to look up in a dictionary he said, "So as much as I'd like to teach you the ropes, and as serendipitous as all this seems to be, I'm afraid I have to ask you to leave."

I finally found some words.

"You mean right now? Today?"

"I'm afraid so. Yes. But I'll write you up a reference as best I can and perhaps you can start fresh somewhere else."

I squeezed the sharp end of my newly lit cigarette between thumb and forefinger, putting it out and then back in its packet. It was time to ration them again because who knew when I'd get another paycheck?

He gave me an envelope with the reference sealed inside, and a cheque that I cashed at the local bank.

After throwing my few things into my suitcase, I hit the road, hitch-hiked back to Picton, caught the ferry and then the train, walked the mile to the family home, and in through the door.

"What are YOU doing here?" said a very surprised mother.

"Got fired. Again," I said.

"Oh! Really! Well, you can't stay here forever. You need to get a job."

With that, for the first time in my life, she really surprised me.

She said, "Do you still want to be a writer, or a reporter?"

"Of course."

The surprise was that she said, "I'll see what I can do."

"Yeah, right!" I thought. "You've never helped me yet."

But I kept those thoughts to myself.

Chapter 56

The Daily News

MUCH TO MY SURPRISE, a week or two later, I came home from a day on the mangolds to have my mother tell me, "We have an interview in New Plymouth."

"What?"

"With the Editor of the Taranaki Daily News."

This time, I was a little older and wiser. Not much older and wiser, but considering my past three experiences with editors, I had learned a thing or two.

Mr. Roche, editor of the Manawatu Times, had fired me for swearing.

The Editor of the Christchurch Star had been pleasant and helpful.

Although visibly taken aback by my ming blue jeans, pinkish shirt, and studded wingtip shoes, the editor of the Westport News had given me a fair shake. He was good enough to send me on my way with a halfway decent but honest reference.

It went something like this.

"Mr. Bill Knight has been with the Westport News for a short time. He has much yet to learn, but was diligent in covering assignments. I wish him all the best in his future endeavors."

In today's world, where it is essential to spend several years acquiring a degree in journalism, a reference like that would probably be a death warrant at any subsequent interview.

However, there was no formal journalism school in New Zealand.

Depending on your future aspirations as a teenager, you would look for an apprenticeship in your preferred field of work. Whether you wanted to be a carpenter, mechanic, or seamstress (as my sister chose to be), you started by approaching established local businesses to see if they had any vacancies. If they did, you could expect to be interviewed, with about a 50/50 chance of being taken on, or not.

Alternatively, you might be fortunate enough to have parents who knew someone in the trade you wanted to follow. I got the job as a copyholder on the Manawatu Times because my father talked with the editor, Mr. Roche.

Now here I was, with my mother having somehow arranged an interview with the editor of a daily paper almost 100 miles from Feilding.

I never asked how she did it, but I'll always be grateful.

By now, my mother had somewhat forgiven me for frying the engine in her '38 Chevy a couple of years previously. It wasn't my fault, of course. It was just that a '38 Chevy was never designed to go over 50 miles an hour in second gear, which I had tried, to see if it would. It wouldn't. It just screamed and died.

I walked five miles home to tell my mother the car had quit on the road near Bunnythorpe. Survival dictates that some truths are best delivered as half truths. "I dunno what happened. The engine just went funny," I said, telling her the absolute truth but not the whole truth.

According to Byron, in whom I confided on pain of death, at such high revs, it was guaranteed that the engine would blow up. He said something called a conrod that connected to something called a piston inside what was known as a block had broken and smashed its way out of the block and the engine died an instant death.

"You should learn to change gears by the sound of the engine and the speed you're doing," he advised in his big-brotherly way. "You certainly don't need to red-line the engine, ever," he added, "and make darn sure you've always got enough oil in the crankcase. And learn to double de-clutch. And if you ever get any good, you'll be able to do doughnuts and handbrake turns."

I didn't understand a word he was saying, but it turned out that he was quite prophetic.

How my mother could afford a replacement engine, I'll never know. She didn't even ask me to chip in. She was also quite okay with me driving as well, so I was on my best driving behavior as we made the trip to New Plymouth.

Passing the mighty but dormant volcano, Mt Egmont, (since renamed as Mt Taranaki) as we neared the city, I was reminded of a Maori prophecy.

For eons, they have said there would come a time when it would rejoin with a trio of major and occasionally active volcanoes in the center of the

North Island. Their names are Ruapehu, Tongariro and Ngauruahoe. As the crow flies, they are 81 miles from Mt Egmont (aka Mt Taranaki).

It hasn't happened yet, but the Maori side of me, and my study of their ancient ways, knowing some of their elders could foresee coming events, tells me this is entirely possible.

It's not as if the volcanoes will just get up and walk toward each other. The logical point of view is that because New Zealand sits atop many fault lines and vast reservoirs of magma, a combination of earthquakes and eruptions could certainly join the volcanoes by flowing rivers of lava.

Once we arrived in New Plymouth, the offices of The Taranaki Daily News were easy enough to find.

Recalling the startled look on the face of the editor at the Westport News when I walked through the door in my Elvis attire, I had dressed a lot more sedately for this interview.

The editor, Mr. Fullarton, was dressed casually in a comfortable-looking but well-worn wool cardigan under which he sported a white shirt and tie. Nicotine staining on his right hand fingers and an ashtray full of cigarette butts indicated he had been in the business for many years.

His left eyebrow only raised about a quarter of an inch as he read my very short paper about my education and journalistic background, and then the reference from the Westport News.

Apparently, he was impressed by my having been co-Dux at Lytton Street school. He asked me a few questions, and I was honest about being fired by Mr. Roche. He listened intently as I told him of my foray to Christchurch looking for work on the Christchurch Star, and what little time I had been in Westport. Perhaps it all spoke to him of determination, which it was.

I was determined to become a reporter.

It is doubtful whether today's editors would even think about what Mr. Fullarton chose to do then.

He changed tack.

He turned to my mother and asked her a few questions about our family circumstances.

Recognizing this as my first opportunity to watch a professional journalist conduct an interview, I sat back and observed.

Within a few minutes, he had learned that Dad was somewhere else and not sending enough money back home.

Going down the sibling list, my mother let him know there were six kids in the family. Byron was away doing an apprenticeship in aircraft engineering. I was currently picking up jobs here and there as a farm laborer around Feilding. What I earned was a big help with the family finances. Marie was living in Palmerston North, where she was an apprentice seamstress. My brother Don was living and working on a dairy farm (learning everything he needed to know in his lifelong future in the dairy industry). And the two youngest, Geoff and Roger, were still at home and going to school, except for working during the school holidays to bring in a little extra cash for the family.

If you're an astute and older reader, you might be tempted to think that she played him like a fiddle. Perish that thought; my thought has always been that he was a caring and honorable man because, much to our complete surprise, he sat back and said nothing.

He stubbed out one cigarette, ejected another filter tip from the pack in his shirt pocket, tapped the filter on the desktop, struck a match, lit the cigarette, inhaled, and like Gandalf the Wizard, slowly exhaled a smoke ring.

The smoke didn't turn into a sailing ship, but the silence seemed to last as long as an ocean journey.

I took note of the smoke ring trick while my mother seemed to find it necessary to examine the outside of the handbag on her knees. She kept turning it back and forth as if to ensure the flap was adequately fastened.

I thought about lighting a cigarette myself, but I only had "rollies" (roll-your-own tobacco and papers) in my jacket pocket, so that was a non-starter.

Allowing the suspense to build for as long as he could, Mr. Fullarton thumbed through the notes he had taken.

Finally, he looked up and spoke to my mother.

"Thank you for bringing your son to see me, Mrs. Knight," he said. "I believe we can find a place for this young man."

The only thing I could come up with as a response was a huge and embarrassing red-faced blush and a very self-conscious silly grin.

He looked at me and smiled. But he wasn't finished yet.

Turning back to my mother, he said, "and by the way, the paper has a policy of helping with relocation expenses. We will gladly pay your shifting costs if you want to find a house or property to rent up here in New Plymouth."

Right then, Mr. Fullarton gained my everlasting respect.

Not only had he shown genuine compassion for us as a family, he had ensured that my career as a reporter was finally getting started.

Chapter 57

Celebration

MY BEST FRIEND IN Feilding at the time was Rick McCall. His mother was editor of the Feilding Herald, and he was learning the basics of journalism.

Rick and I got along very well, and on the drive back home, I could think of no better person to celebrate with.

Alistair Williams had gone on to Teacher Training College. Ivan Horbun and I had drifted apart. I no longer had anything to do with Tony Boyle. All of which is evidence that friends come and go in life, according to your mutual interests.

Our mutual interests often required a trip to Palmerston North in his little Prefect car.

These missions would take us to the small milk bar where a banana split with ice cream and a sit down with two or more of the local girls made for a great night out. Sometimes a couple of girlfriends would agree to a ride home to their place. Rick would gallantly open the front passenger door and, with a bow and sweep of his arm, invite the lady of his preference to sit alongside him.

Not being a slow learner, I worked the same technique for the rear seat. It always worked like a charm. Seldom would any of them make a fuss if perchance Rick took a wrong turn and the car somehow found itself parked in a dark spot in The Esplanade.

Milk shakes are one thing. Beer is another, and home brew beer is something else again. We graduated from milkshakes to beer on those occasional visits to The Esplanade. Beer seemed to lighten me up and dissolve any of my barriers of shyness. I became a happy loquacious nice guy, which is what led to a fight that came close to having me killed.

Rick picked me up one Friday evening. Under my arm, I had the usual brown paper bag containing two bottles of DB Lager, quart size. Rick's two quarts were in a similar bag on the floor in front of the passenger seat.

"Careful with those," he said, as I started to place them all on the floor. "They're home brew."

"What? Where'd you get them?"

"My brother makes his own. He let me have a couple. There's one each." Rick was generous like that.

Now that we knew the value of beer on our Friday night outings, we had adopted the habit of drinking a bottle each before changing into our irresistible personas and downsizing to milkshakes and trophy hunting.

Yes, that's a crude way to put it, but have I said anything about the night we introduced ourselves to two young ladies in the milk bar? Rick started with his usual suave line, "Hello. What are you doing tonight?" One of them smiled, raised an eyebrow, and in a seductive whisper replied, "Trophy hunting." We all laughed. We had reached an immediate understanding.

It was a great night, and Rick and I would often laugh and use the term thereafter.

Chapter 58

Do Or Die

As we left for Palmerston, I cracked the tops off the two bottles of home brew. Driving one-handed and swigging from his bottle, Rick said, "I hear there's a party up the river at Pohangina. Wanna go?"

Interrupting my own guzzling, I responded, "Why not? Yeah."

On the way, I discovered that a bottle of home brew could make me twice as happy as any quart of DB Lager ever had. The only drawback was the sediment at the bottom. It was disgusting. I had to open the DB to get that taste out of my mouth.

The party, complete with a blazing bonfire, was well under way when we arrived. It had been quite a drive from Feilding to Totara Park and the bridge over the Pohangina river. We got there some time after dark.

Rick parked a little distance from the fire. Not seeing anyone we knew, we decided to sit alongside the car and drink the rest of our beer.

I'm not sure whether it was the beer bottles, or us, that soon attracted two teenage girls. They approached, smiled, and, without being asked, sat themselves down on either side of us - each within arm's reach of a beer bottle.

We engaged in chitchat about nothing meaningful for quite a while, reflecting on the beauty of the moon and stars and the benefits of home brew and DB. Rick had been sneaky enough to hide two extra bottles in the car, which we gallantly offered to share with our new companions. Naturally, they were grateful.

My chatter-boxing seemed to impress the girl alongside me. She kept giggling at my comments - then suddenly stopped in mid-giggle. The moon had disappeared.

I looked up.

Between me and the moon was an enormous person dressed like a soldier.

He spoke.

"Get in the trees!"

Puzzled, I said, "What?"

"Get in the trees. She's my girlfriend."

What did that have to do with getting in the trees?

"Whad- for?" I slurred.

"I'm SAS," he snapped, very loudly. "I'm gonna teach you a lesson."

"Oh shid! Spacial Air Service I thought. And he wants a fight? What for? I don't. I'm just having a good time.

I did not want a fight. I wanted to be happy and chatty. I had had no intention of moving in on his girlfriend... or maybe I had, since she had said nothing about having a boyfriend there.

I tried the soft sell approach. "Here. Have a beer. Settle down."

It did no good. His voice got louder each time he demanded that I "get in the trees."

Ah well, you can only resist an invitation to a fight for so long.

I stood up, somewhat shakily, and followed him into a small clearing among the trees, not far from the fire. Alerted by his loud shouting, the rest of the party-goers followed to form a circle. They knew, which I did not, that fights were not uncommon at such gatherings.

As I had done in my few prior boxing bouts, I took my place at one side of the circle. He stood opposite. Rick was off to one side. I watched them all appearing and disappearing in the alternating light and dark of the flickering flames.

Boxers stay on their feet in a fight, feinting and striking and dancing back and forth. That's fine in a boxing ring with a level floor. Among trees whose pine needles have formed a deep carpet, it is not good at all. It is especially not good against a soldier who has been trained to fight very dirty, and fight to kill.

To his credit, he did first engage in boxing mode. He probably expected to knock me out in front of his girlfriend and put a quick end to the fight. It didn't happen.

However, I can take no accolades for my performance. I was drunk, groggy, and uncoordinated. So much so that I was weaving like a drunk (did I say that?) and throwing punches in a hit and miss manner. One of them went wild and wide enough to hit someone on the sideline on the side of his face. (I think that was Rick, although he never mentioned it later).

If I landed any hits on this soldier, I might as well have been punching a brick.

My next memory blip is that he closed in, got some sort of hold I had never heard of, did a hip throw or a trip maneuver and there I was, face down with this SAS guy straddling my back.

I was helpless.

This was certainly not going well.

The impact of the side of his right fist on the back of my neck drove my face into the cushion of needles. I had a momentary vision of myself doing exactly that to finish off rabbits. It was called a rabbit chop.

Chop!

Chop!

Chop!

Deeper and deeper went my head into the pine needles.

I could now feel the bones in my neck separating.

He was trying to kill me, and as the blows rained down, I knew he would not stop until I was dead.

Who knows how I did it? If you've seen men doing push-ups, I'll bet you've never seen one do it with a 200-pound gorilla on his back.

I did it.

Caught by surprise, he fell backwards.

I jumped to my feet, spun around, and there he was, on his knees, looking at me with absolute astonishment.

There is a time for no mercy.

This was it.

I stepped in, grabbed an ear in each hand, pulled his head up, and smashed my right knee full force into his face.

Guess what!

He stayed on his knees and started crying. Really crying. And blubbering. "He kicked me in the face! He kicked me in the face!"

This fight was over. I glanced around the group of strangers. Was one of them a friend of this guy and ready to go another round or two?

Fortunately, No.

Rick and I headed for the car, surprised to see we were being followed by the two girls we had been chatting with earlier.

"Can you take us home?" asked one. "He's NOT my boyfriend," said the other.

There was no chitter-chatter on that journey. None. And no stopping at The Esplanade either. Their parents were no doubt very surprised when their daughters arrived home long before their midnight deadline.

Shortly thereafter, it was time to head to New Plymouth for a fresh start in my new career.

It was agreed that my mother and brothers (Geoff and Roger) should remain in Feilding until I had found a big enough place for us in New Plymouth.

Before long, I was renting a room in a widow's New Plymouth home.

I was almost 19 years old.

Chapter 59

Epilogue

A S A LIFELONG JOURNALIST I learned long ago that there is always
more to the story, and so it is. This book is only part of the story of
my life.

As a quick review of what I have covered so far, you'll recall how, with no
conscious intention, I catapulted or teleported to safety. That happened
when I was running for my life, then tripped in front of a stampeding herd
of cattle. I blinked and was instantly behind the concrete trough in the next
field.

Then there was the moment I "walked on water" while again running for
my life, this time across that driftwood logjam on Hughie's farm.

Remember my hypnotized friend Alistair, lying horizontally with his head
on one chair and feet on another, and nothing underneath to support him
at al all, how did the mind allow that to happen?

My later use of self-hypnosis to get that hole shot in motocross got me
wondering even further about the mysteries of the mind.

My questions about religion and the bible and on into atheism were and
are genuine events and experience. They are the truth. But they do not tell

the full story of my journey through atheism and out the other side, with a whole new understanding of God.

I will be working on the next volume as soon as this one is published - in fact, it may already be published by the time you read this.

You might also consider subscribing to my free newsletter at www.northstarnewsletter.com. And while there, perhaps take a look at what is available in the shop - including several free reports in PDF format. They deal with current events in the world, in quite a different way and style than I have used to relate this personal journey.

Reviews play a very significant role in potential buyers deciding which of several titles in the same genre to buy. Therefore, if you bought this book from Amazon, or elsewhere online, it would be much appreciated if you would return there and pen a review; in your own words, of course.

Yours Sincerely,

Michael Knight.

About The Author

Michael Knight

Michael Knight is a retired (now 77) award-winning reporter and writer/author.

He started his career in New Zealand in 1960. After seven years on newspapers he moved on to radio, and thence to national television news.

Over the course of three decades he covered assignments in Australia, the UK, Canada and the United States of America.

In Australia for several years he worked in Public Relations for Hamersley Iron in Dampier, Western Australia, and then as a newsreader at TVW7/6IX in Perth.

Returning to New Zealand and to network television, , which saw the establishment of two national channels (TVOne and TVTwo) he worked for TVOne as a reporter, and as a national editor supervising staff throughout the country.

Knight also established a news camera business and spent two years as a cameraman before returning to TVOne as a reporter and Director for the ever-popular Country Calendar weekly program.

Having lived by the ethics of the trade since his first years on newspapers, he left the radio and television news business after one copy editor altered one of his scripts, saying "never let the facts spoil a good story."

Another television news editor insisted he go and interview a bereaved mother whose daughter had died in a tragic accident. "And if she isn't crying on camera," said the editor, "I won't use the story."

Knight refused the assignment and handed in his resignation soon after.

His first book, "Building With Logs in New Zealand," co-authored with his ex-partner Liz Brook, sold out in both Canada and New Zealand.

Knight moved to the United States in 1990, and is a naturalized citizen of the US.

He has written seven books since – including this one. Five are now out of print.

Still available at time of writing is a book he wrote and published in 2017 – *"President Trump and the New World Order – The Ramtha Trump Prophecy."*

There's a short story behind that.

After quitting the corrupt mainstream media, Knight worked on contract or researched and wrote articles for various magazines. In 1987 he learned about the star of the then top-rated "Dynasty" program in the US. The yellow press of the tme were saying she was involved in a "cult" based in Yelm, Washington, where a woman was purportedly "channeling" an ancient warrior called Ramtha The Enlightened One.

As Knight puts it, "You have to go there to know there. While my growing interest in spiritual matters was part of my decision, I also thought I could make a lot of money if I were to attend an event, prove it was all fraudulent, and sell the article worldwide.

"I had to see for myself and decide for myself because I prefer to make up my own mind.

"To that end I paid my own way to an event.

"After the morning session I said something about it to my partner while we were having lunch in our rented RV. After lunch, Ramtha looked in our direction and repeated what I had said, word for word.

"While I still did not understand how a woman could "channel," that – and further follow-up trips from New Zealand – were proof enough that this was not a fraud.

"I moved to Yelm in 1990 to continue my education, through which I have found answers to the many questions I had been pondering since childhood.

"I have gladly paid for my education over the years, as one does when attending a university; this one just happens to be a school of the mind."

The organisation is registered as The Ramtha School of Enlightenment.

www.ramtha.com.

The book, *"President Trump and the New World Order,"* is available in print and eBook versions on Amazon.

https://amzn.to/3H4eBoR

You can subscribe to his current newsletter, the North Star Newsletter (free) at www.northstarnewsletter.com.